Identity, Theory, and Practice in Group Relations

Identity, Theory, and Practice in Group Relations presents a range of perspectives on group relations, capturing both a social scientific and psychoanalytic perspective.

Each chapter explores themes of identity, theory, and practice, where the process of looking at others and oneself is amplified, and the task of exploring the space we occupy is changed. *Identity, Theory and Practice in Group Relations* includes discussion of critical race theory, corruption, Black leadership and sibling relations, the role of technology and how it has been adopted and adapted by group relations practitioners, as well as specific perspectives on group relations in Italy and China and reflections on group relations through the COVID-19 pandemic.

This book will be an invaluable resource for practitioners, academics and scholars of Group Relations, as well as managers and organisational members wanting to learn more about how Groups Relations methods can contribute to their organisational success.

Coreene Archer is a principal consultant and executive coach at the Tavistock Institute, UK. Coreene's interests lie in the study of leadership and identity. Her work has expanded group relations ideas to include work with emergent and young leaders. Coreene teaches on several programmes at both the Institute and externally.

Gordon Strauss is a former board member and treasurer of the A. K. Rice Institute (AKRI) and former director of the AKRI National Conference. He represented the AKRI on the Belgirate Management and Administrative Team from 2014–2024. He is Emeritus Professor of Psychiatry at the University of Louisville, USA.

Moshe Bergstein is a training psychoanalyst at the Israel Psychoanalytic Society. He teaches and supervises at the Psychoanalytic Institute and in various psychoanalytic psychotherapy programmes. He studies and publishes on the work of W. R. Bion, and the interface between psychoanalysis and the arts.

Ellen L. Short was Professor at Long Island University, author, and consultant, who was an active member of the A. K. Rice Institute and the New York Centre for the Study of Groups, Organizations and Social Systems. She died in May of 2024.

The Group Relations Conferences Series

Group Relations conferences offer opportunities to learn about group, organisational and social dynamics; the exercise of authority and power; the interplay between tradition, innovation and change; and the relationship of organisations to their social, political and economic environments This series of books on the Tavistock Group Relations Conferences provides edited collections of papers presented at the Belgirate conferences, plus additional chapters which examine the respective conference as a whole.
Titles in the series:

Group Relations Conferences
Tradition, Creativity, and Succession in the Global Group Relations Network: Volume III
Edited by Eliat Aram, Robert Baxter and Avi Nutkevitch

Adaptation and Innovation
Theory, Design and Role-Taking in Group Relations Conferences and their Applications: Volume II
Edited by Eliat Aram, Robert Baxter and Avi Nutkevitch

Group Relations Conferences
Reviewing and Exploring Theory, Design, Role-Taking and Application
Edited by Louisa Diana Brunner, Avi Nutkevitch and Mannie Sher

Identity, Theory, and Practice in Group Relations
A Reflective Selfie
Edited by Coreene Archer, Gordon Strauss, Moshe Bergstein and Ellen L. Short

For further information about this series please visit: https://www.routledge.com/The-Group-Relations-Conferences-Series/book-series/KARNGRC

Identity, Theory, and Practice in Group Relations

A Reflective Selfie

Edited by
Coreene Archer, Gordon Strauss,
Moshe Bergstein and Ellen L. Short

Routledge
Taylor & Francis Group
LONDON AND NEW YORK

Designed cover image: © Getty Images

First published 2026
by Routledge
4 Park Square, Milton Park, Abingdon, Oxon OX14 4RN

and by Routledge
605 Third Avenue, New York, NY 10158

Routledge is an imprint of the Taylor & Francis Group, an informa business

British Library Cataloguing-in-Publication Data
A catalogue record for this book is available from the British Library

ISBN: 9781032819198 (hbk)
ISBN: 9781032812618 (pbk)
ISBN: 9781003502050 (ebk)

DOI: 10.4324/9781003502050

Typeset in Times New Roman
by codeMantra

Contents

About the contributors

Smadar Ashuach is a clinical psychologist, supervisor, training psychoanalyst and group analyst. She is a member teacher and supervisor at Tel-Aviv Institute of Contemporary Psychoanalysis and the Israeli Institute of Group Analysis. Head of Group Psychotherapy Program at the School of Psychoanalytic Psychotherapy, School of Medicine, Tel Aviv University. She is a co-author (with Avi Berman) of *Sibling Relations and the Horizontal Axis in Theory and Practice.* A member of OFEK, she lives and practises in Israel. smadar.ashuach@gmail.com

Louisa Diana Brunner, PhD, Leadership and Management Consultant, Executive Coach, Advanced Practice Lead and Senior Lecturer Tavistock and Portman Professional Doctorate and Certificate in Consultation and the Organisation; Faculty Member Family Business Institute Global Education Network; Member OFEK, OPUS, ISPSO, Founding Member PCCA, Honorary Member Il Nodo Group.

Claudio Cassardo (Editor), Head of the operational unit for psychological patient support at the San Paolo and San Carlo H, Milan. Ordinary Member of the Italian Psychoanalytic Society (SPI) and International Psychoanalytic Society (IPA). Member of the Il Nodo Group.

Pietro Catania, Social scientist with a Stanford background, Professor of Management at Milano Bicocca University, and MBA from Bocconi University. Founder of Alef Consulting and Ayros Press. Tavistock Institute alumnus, iG-OLD graduate, and recipient of the NTL Institute's "Edie Seashore Award" for commitment to Social Justice. Co-founder of Dialogic Effect and Palladia.

Elyce Cole, is a senior researcher–practitioner at the TIHR and specialises in group dynamics through a systems psychodynamic lens. She focuses on organisational issues tied to power, authority, and group identity at the team level, particularly within virtual teams. Her expertise includes advising global public health, education, and tech sectors on improving team effectiveness for diverse teams. She is Board Vice President (2023–present) of the NY Center for the study of groups, organisations, and social systems that brings together a diverse community of devoted professionals and students learning about group relations.

Shmuel Erlich, Ph.D., is a clinical psychologist; training and supervising psychoanalyst and past president of the Israel Psychoanalytic Society; consultant to organizations; Sigmund Freud Professor of Psychoanalysis (Emeritus), The Hebrew University of Jerusalem; Co-Founder of OFEK, and Co-Founder and current chair of PCCA. He received the Sigourney Award in 2005 for outstanding contributions to psychoanalysis and is the author of three books and numerous publications.

Mira Erlich-Ginor, M.A., is a clinical psychologist and training and supervising psychoanalyst of the Israel Psychoanalytic Society. She is deeply involved in psychoanalytic education and Group Relations work and committed to the application of psychoanalytic understandings to societal issues. She is currently Chair of the Steering Committee, IPA in the Community and the World. She is Co-Founder and past chair of OFEK; Co-Founder of the "Nazareth Project," Group Relations work on transgenerational transmission of trauma; and Co-founder of PCCA, Partners in Confronting Collective Atrocities, which is the recipient of the Sigourney Award 2019.

Franca Fubini is a psychoanalytic psychotherapist, group analyst, supervisor and organisational consultant. Member, consultant and director of Group Relations conferences. With Lawrence and Baglioni, introduced Social Dreaming in Italy and developed the first social dreaming training for hosts. Host of Reflective Citizenship and of Listening Posts. Chair of Social Dreaming international Network (SDiN), a Member of OPUS and of ISPSO, and former associate Chair of il Nodo Group.

Mary Fullerton, EMBA, is a Tavistock-trained change consultant (P3C; Dynamics at Board Level) and an iPEC-certified executive coach. She is Co-founder of Caribbean Group Relations Consulting (CGRC), advancing systems psychodynamics in leadership and organisational development. From 2018 to 2024, she curated and staffed Caribbean Group Relations conferences. Mary is Managing Director of The Buzz Limited, an advertising agency, and Founder/CEO of the ADHD Foundation of Trinidad and Tobago, an advocate for inclusive systems and neurodiversity. She values time with family, intercultural travel, and continuous learning in emerging sciences and technology.

Chiara Ghetti is a psychiatrist, psychoanalyst, and an Associate Member IPA/SPI. She worked for 20 years in public psychiatry and drug addiction services in Emilia Romagna and she is currently a private practitioner. Group leader in social and healthcare sectors, she supervises mental health teams at the Bologna Local Health Authority. She conducts group training in psychotherapy for psychiatric residents of the University of Bologna and in clinical communication at a training course in General Medicine. She collaborates with PER Group (European Psychoanalysts for Refugees).

Matthew Gieve is a senior social research and consultant at the Tavistock Institute, working predominantly in the area of complex programme evaluation, specialising in the fields of children social care and mental health. He is also a Group Relations practitioner and teaches on a number of professional development programmes. As a researcher and consultant drawing on his background in psychoanalytic theory, psychology, and social science, he has worked on projects relating to social care, including family separation and, more recently, organisational well-being, managing a learning process with an international programme aimed at improving staff well-being in the social change sector.

Robert C. Hsiung MD is a psychiatrist in private practice; a co-founder and past president of the International Society for Mental Health Online; the editor of *E-Therapy: Case Studies, Guiding Principles, and the Clinical Potential of the Internet* (Norton, 2002); and the founder of Psycho-Babble, a large public online peer support group.

Urban Hudlin, O.P. is a Dominican priest, psychoanalytic psychotherapist, and organisational consultant. He is Co-founder of Caribbean Group Relations Consulting, which hosted its first Group Relations Conference in 2018 in association with the Tavistock Institute, London. He did his doctoral work at Catholic Theological Union, Chicago, and completed training in psychoanalytic psychotherapy at the School of Medicine, University College Dublin. He also holds advanced certification in Group Relations, Consultancy, and Change, and Dynamics at Board Level from the Tavistock Institute. His work integrates theology, psychology, and systems thinking, focusing on leadership development, pastoral renewal, and organisational transformation.

Manuela Martelli MD, is a psychotherapist specialising in medical psychology and neurology, a psychoanalyst and associated member of the Italian Psychoanalytic Association and the International Psychoanalytic Association. A trainer for the Local Health Authority and the University of Bologna, she has been leading clinical and supervision groups for several years, both with social service workers (of elderly rehabilitation facilities and in the reception services for asylum seekers and holders of international protection) and in the healthcare field (mental health professionals, general practitioners, medical students). From 2017 to 2021, she has been working as psychotherapist for the Bologna Local Health Authority, taking care of migrants with psychological and psychiatric difficulties.

Luca Mingarelli is a social entrepreneur and psychologist. Ideator of Democratic Therapeutic Communities for adolescents (1998). Past president Il Nodo Group. Director/consultant of international GRCs. Ideator and Director LFA and GRC ECW. Organisational consultant.

Dr Maria Pia Conte is a psychiatrist and psychoanalyst SPI, IPA. She worked in psychiatric hospitals and for institutes for deaf children before their closure. She worked in the Italian NHS for 20 years for bilingual development of deaf children and recognition of the deaf community as a linguistic minority. She is also a consultant for women's shelters. She is staff of Group Relations Conferences and Member of Social Dreaming International Network. Past President Centro Psicoanalitico di Genova, Guest member British Psychoanalytic Society, Member IPA Violence Committee and Observatory on Gender Violence SPI.

Francesco Noseda is a psychologist, psychotherapist, and IFPS psychoanalyst, and organizational consultant with Il Nodo Group. He provides supervision and consultancy in complex clinical and institutional settings internationally, grounded in a systemic -psychodynamic model. He teaches and holds scientific roles in Group Relations Conferences. Author on adolescence, groups, and institutions.

Jeffrey D. Roth, MD CGP FAGPA is an addiction psychiatrist; a director of Group Relations Conferences for the AK Rice Institute and Virtual Large Study Groups for an international consortium of group relations organizations; a past president of the Chicago Center for the Study of Groups and Organizations; a past editor of the *Journal of Groups in Addiction and Recovery*; and the director of WorkingSobriety.com

Antonio Sama is a university academic and organisational consultant. He is a professional partner of the Tavistock Institute of Human Relations. His interests include the role of systemic psychodynamics in university education, action research and complexity and change processes in the third sector. Antonio holds roles in Italian and British universities

Yael Shenhav-Sharoni, M.A., is a clinical psychologist; training and supervising psychoanalyst, Tel-Aviv Institute of Contemporary Psychoanalysis; APsA member, IPA; Consultant to organizations; Member and past-Chair, OFEK.

Sivanie Shiran, PhD is Faculty Head of Leadership Development in the G/MBA programmes, Reichman University, Israel. She is a Jungian psychoanalyst and a clinical psychologist in private practice, and consults to senior executives from multinational corporations at the Institute for Management Development (IMD) in Switzerland and to leading civil servants at the Wexner Foundation, Israel. She is a board member of OFEK.

Simi Talmi M.S.W. is a training psychoanalyst and organisational consultant. Former Chair of Tel Aviv institution of Contemporary Psychoanalysis; former co-director of the Program in Organization Consultation & Development: A Psychoanalytic-Systemic Approach, Ofek member.

Rossella Torretta is a clinical psychologist, psychotherapist, psychoanalyst and supervisor. She is an expert in psychoanalytic psychodrama and a trainer and group conductor. She studies group interactions with their dynamics and the roles taken by subjects within organisations and institutional realities. She is also a supervisor in migrant and mother–infants' communities. Il Nodo Group, SIPRe and IFPS associated.

Joseph (Yossi) Triest, Ph.D., is a clinical psychologist, training and supervising psychoanalyst and organisational consultant. He was president of the Israel Psychoanalytic Society; Currently, heads the "Freud and Followers Track" at the Tel-Aviv University Psychotherapy Program, and is on faculty at Tel Aviv University Sackler Medical School PhD program. He is co-founder and co-director of the Triest-Sarig Psychotherapy Clinic, and co-director of the Center for Research of the Psychoanalytic-Systemic Approach. is a Member of OFEK; was a member of the MAT and is co-author of several Belgirate books and publications.

Elio Vera is a communications expert, honorary member of IL NODO Group, founder and honorary president of CESMA Executive Education, member emeritus of EFMD. He is a member of OPUS Organization for Promoting Understanding of Society. In May 2022, he was appointed President of the IAGP Ethics and Professional Standards Committee. Past member of the board of directors of SIETAR EUROPA intercultural exchange, research, development. Past Executive Corner Editor on the editorial board of Cross Cultural Management. Past member of ISPSO. Past president of the Technical Scientific Committee of AFORISMA Business School.

Dorothee C. von Tippelskirch-Eissing, Dr Phil, Dipl Psych, has studied Protestant theology and psychology. She works as a psychoanalyst in private practice in Berlin, Germany. She is a supervisor and training analyst of the German Psychoanalytic Association (DPV) and the International Psychoanalytical Association (IPA). She is the president of the German Psychoanalytic Association (DPV/IPA). She is a member and former chairperson of the Karl-Abraham-Institute, Berlin Psychoanalytic Institute (BPI), member and former chairperson of the board of Partners in Confronting Collective Atrocities (PCCA).

Joseph E. Wise MD CGP is a certified group psychotherapist and Board-certified psychiatrist practising in Brooklyn; an Army psychiatrist for a decade, including in Iraq in 2010; an author and presenter on psychodynamic and interpersonal group therapy approaches to working with military/Veterans and treating combat PTSD; a co-editor of *Gay Mental Healthcare: Providers and Patients in the Military* (Springer, 2018); and a former Chief of Behavioral Health at a military community hospital.

Foreword

Mannie Sher

Since 1957, Group Relations Conferences have been educational events which are based on learning through experience. Participants in Group Relations Conferences study and learn about the strategic and structural dynamics of organisations from a psychoanalytic-systemic perspective. The knowledge is acquired and then applied by working through the conscious and unconscious dynamics of leadership and management in groups, organisations and systems. Group Relations Conferences have been adapted and modified over the years as a laboratory of reflection in various local contexts, including the social, cultural, religious, spiritual, geographical and theoretical.

Since 2003, the Belgirate scientific meetings have become a meta-study hub where staff practitioners of Group Relations Conferences come together to share, explore and reflect upon the theory, practice, discourse and values of the Group Relations field and the changes that have taken place over time.

Belgirate VII focused on the identity of group relations practitioners and theoretical discourse and practice. In that sense, Belgirate VII offered an opportunity for a "Selfie": an invitation to the "family" of Group Relations practitioners to reflect on their work and professional community. What is the nature of Group Relations reflective methods? What do we see? What would a "tourist" see? Belgirate VII made a "Selfie" of the current state of the Group Relations community by exploring the lived experience of its identity, theory, and practice. Naturally, the Group Relations community could not ignore the influence of the pandemic in the way group relations conferences are designed and delivered.

This is another wonderful book of the proceedings of the latest, the 7th, International Conference on Group Relations, held in the beautiful small town of Belgirate on the shores of Lake Maggiore, Italy. The Belgirate conference is a four-day residential conference held every three years for people who have held staff roles at Group Relations Conferences that are conducted in the Tavistock tradition. I need to say this because Tavistock-style Group Relations Conferences and other types of conferences involving group work are very different things altogether. One of the aims of the Belgirate conference is to seek to identify the uniqueness of Tavistock Group Relations Conferences – what they are, and what they are not.

First, what is a Group Relations Conference in the Tavistock tradition and how does it differ from other group-based conferences, training events or educational activities? And why do we have an international conference for those who work in this field?

I will begin with a personal note: I was the Director of the Tavistock Institute of Human Relations' Group Relations Programme from 1997 to 2017, and in this role, in partnership with Avi Nutkevitch of OFEK, Israel, we founded the Belgirate conference in 2003. Hence, it seems fitting and a great privilege to have been asked by the Belgirate VII Management & Administrative Team (Coreene Archer, Moshe Bergstein, Seth Harkins, Rachel Kelly, Gordon Strauss, and Joseph Triest) to write the Foreword to this volume.

Like the giants in the field of Group Relations – Ken Rice and Eric Miller – my role was to assist groups of people in many parts of the world build their own Group Relations institutions and eventually to staff their group relations conferences. Since the inception of Group Relations conferences, about 25 group relations institutions were established, or sprung up spontaneously, to promote a unique form of learning about the nature and complexities of groups, about participation of individuals in group learning, by consistently focusing on the deeper underlying group dynamics, philosophies, and relationships that groups mobilise, sometimes for good purposes and sometimes for defensive reasons. Putting it another way, the conferences on Group Relations offer a unique opportunity for those wishing to study group dynamics to examine the state of Group Relations Conference work around the world, provide participants with the opportunity of considering afresh unconscious influences on group behaviour that are rooted in history and culture. And, whether experienced in this method or not, to help see and work with a group's defences, by actively participating experientially in the events of the conference and abandoning the usual spectator role or the role of the silent member of a passive audience. The aim of the Belgirate Group Relations conferences is to penetrate to deeper levels the mysteries of the life of groups of which one is a working member. In pursuit of this task, groups will be formed, and they will work without the usual allocation of experienced consultants as would happen in regular Group Relations Conferences. This self-managing aspect to group work is adopted because "training" in a technique can paradoxically have strong defensive qualities that subvert the process of learning. Group Relations is watchful against anything that interferes with learning about the self-justifications, delusions and dark corners of human nature, wherein also lie, surprisingly, sources of creative ideas and drives that encourage the human spirit to keep learning about itself while engaging consciously and cognitively with the world at large. I am alluding here to the conflict between the group unconscious – those thoughts, feelings, and phantasies about the group's behaviour, and the group's engagement with its social, technical, and ethical tasks. A good example might be the ideas we all repress about unsustainable consumption, which we deny, distancing ourselves from feelings of guilt and responsibility, or from having to take corrective action.

This book exemplifies the growth in the spread of themes that Group Relations Conferences address across the globe. From Sivani Shiran's powerful and moving description of approaching personal loss and its impact on her ability to participate at the Belgirate VII Group Relations Conference – removing herself from the conference experience by "hiding in plain sight", and dealing with the frustrations of virtual relationships when her overpowering need was for closeness and human contact by daring to voice her feelings openly in a group, to Erlich, Sharoni, Erlich-Ginor and Triest's excellent paper on corruption.

In Matt Gieve's and Elyce Coles' insightful paper on their roles as the technical team supporting the virtual technology of the conference they describe how new technology stirs up deep dependency, and how the technical team sought to encourage their colleagues in a more balanced approach through collective problem-solving that proved to yield more effective and sustainable solutions. Gieve and Coles point out that new technologies continually challenge and alter nature and the object of our dependency, influencing every aspect of our lives, extending and enhancing our capacities, offering new-found levels of independence by dispensing with assistance from fellow humans. Belgirate VII, perhaps because it coincided with the COVID-19 pandemic, shows how virtual technology permits greater connection across vast distances and offers the promise of greater human contact, but the barriers presented by the technologies themselves lead to feelings of isolation and loneliness and greater detachment.

The chapter by Jeffrey Roth and his team of American and Chinese consultants describes the momentous task of developing Group Relations Conferences in China; how a cluster of ideas that originated in the West was transplanted in the East. They write about the agonies of the transfer that came with the exposure of a 5,000-year history of understanding human nature and relationships, and its adaptation to the methodology of examining individual thoughts and experiences in a group context. As with many interesting examples in the book, they describe the conflicts and changes in human affairs that led to the building of more than one Chinese Group Relations Conference institution and the development of new networks and the fluidity of knowledge in interdependent endeavour. Of particular interest is their description of the tensions between China, Taiwan, and the USA, and how this historical reality is raising the frightening question of whether the three pivotal players in the broader geopolitics in the region will be able to collaborate or not. Does Group Relations conference work have a role here? Is working with "power" dynamics at international levels merely a step up from working with organisational dynamics? And if so, how would that influence Group Relations conference design? These are important questions raised by this book.

Mary Fullerton's "Too Black to lead" – a chapter on intergroup relations in the political arena of Trinidad & Tobago's national systems (police and army) – describes relationships between the country's current statutory authorities and their origins in the islands' multicultural and multiracial history. They also make the interesting link between the economic needs of the early colonisers that were satisfied through exploitation, domination, and absolute control, which also alienates people from their cultural endowments to this day.

Louisa Brunner's thoughtful piece brings together the postponing of a Group Relations Conference (because of COVID-19) and the music of Simon and Garfunkel, "The Sound of Silence" and Shapiro and Carr's book *Lost in Familiar Places* through her photographs of the empty streets of her hometown, Milan, during the pandemic. Louisa's paper focuses on the trouble connected with the death instinct and the sense of "not being" – how traumatic events relate to the past and cannot be connected to the present, as if it were "an untouchable ghost". The COVID virus is quoted as "the other" that affected Louisa's early experience as the conference director who had to cancel a Group Relations Conference because of the pandemic and the effect of this loss on her identity. It is also referred to as "other" in Smadar and Simi's exploration of sibling relations.

The Management and Administration Team (MAT) of the Belgirate VII conference has produced an informative and educational book about the little-known subject of Group Relations that is punching above its weight in the world of organisational development and making a huge impression in the application of its ideas and methods to fields of human endeavour outside the organisation, in networks and in social and political movements. If you are interested in understanding more of these volatile and hazardous human processes, then you could start with this book, but better still, attend and experience a Group Relations Conference near you.

Introduction

This book, like all the others in the series is based on the Belgirate meetings that take place every three years for anyone who has taken up a staff role in a group relations conference. The meetings have been held in Belgirate, Lago Maggiore in Italy since 2003.

The theme of the meeting was *Group Relations 2021: A Selfie Portraying Our Identity, Theory, & Practice,* as a space to explore the conscious and unconscious assumptions, phantasies, forces and perceptions that shape and influence Group Relations Conferences. Its task was to explore the experience of reflecting on ourselves, what we see, what we notice and how these inform, and are informed by, our lived experience and application in different spaces and contexts.

As we considered the role of social media on society, the idea of a "selfie" seemed like a relevant way to explore the emerging shape of group relations especially with the arrival of online conferences. The *Oxford English Dictionary* defines a selfie as "an image that includes oneself (often with another person or as part of a group) and is taken by oneself using a digital camera especially for posting on social networks".

In group relations, the study of groups and group behaviour is the norm. How individuals show up in groups and are used by groups is our usual unit of measurement. The use of a selfie amplifies and further focuses our lens. The work of the cultural critic John Berger helps us to consider both the act of "looking" and the nature of "seeing" through the medium of the photograph and the role it plays in the wider society. He makes two strong statements that are relevant to the nature of our work: "what we look at is an act of choice" and that an "image" is a moment that has been created or recreated and is detached from the place and time that it was first made. What then, in the use of the group relations methodology, do we choose to see or choose to ignore? What are we drawn to and which parts of us are illuminated by the act of "looking or seeing"?

Perhaps the real preoccupation behind our consideration of the selfie is the question of legacy. What will we add to the canon of the Group Relations field? In his seminal book, *Ways of Seeing* (1972), Berger reminds us that an image can be emotionally charged, as it captures and highlights the human condition. Our response is not neutral, as often so much of what we see corresponds to our own observations.

This fact is also true of group relations, particularly in the online space where so much of what we experience is reduced to only what we can see. Nevertheless, there is a psychological and social urgency that is linked to the experience.

The lens of this book is focused on one of two keynote lectures and three rounds of parallel presentations. In addition, we have included several personal reflective pieces from the participants at the meeting.

We continue to use the definition we've always used in the discourse, which has been consistent across the meetings, and by this we mean the language we use, our terms, our ethical values (explicit or implicit), the nature of the concepts we use in our theoretical writings, our metaphors and their hidden meanings, the tools and methods we use in our practice, the nature of our work – in short, our professional culture.

The book is divided into three parts. Part I focuses on aspects of international perspectives on the ideas of Group Relations and their applications. Part II explores aspects of leadership and how it is experienced in the directorship of Group Relations Conferences and in relation to experiences of Belgirate VII. The book concludes with Part III, which contains reflections from participants who were at the meeting.

As with the previous volumes in this series, chapters in this book are largely based on presentations made at the Belgirate VII meeting. Some of the authors updated their presentations and others refocused their chapters and so the book continues to offer a new lens on a past experience, offering additional opportunities for learning.

Coreene, Gordon, Moshe, and Ellen
Spring 2024

Reference

Berger, J. (1972). *Ways of Seeing*. London: Penguin Classics.

Part I

International Perspectives

Introduction to Part I

Part I explores aspects of international perspectives on the ideas of Group Relations and their applications, in relation to the experiences of Belgirate VII. The chapters in this part share observations on Group Relations (GR) in different cultural contexts, using personal experiences to reflect on larger phenomena.

Dorothee C. von Tippelskirch-Eissing's chapter is based on her keynote lecture at Belgirate VII. She describes the work of Partners in Confronting Collective Atrocities (PCCA), briefly reviewing the history of its activities and previous Belgirate presentations on its work. She describes the specificity of PCCA's work in addressing collective trauma, using GR methodology in order to directly deal with what may be seen as previous unconscious avoidance of dealing with unbearable collective pain while using this same methodology in "regular" Group Relations Conferences. She offers a poignant example in which German training psychoanalysts shared personal painful events in the process of their professional training, which then appeared to present a group symptom. She writes of the work of freeing oneself from processes that tend to get personalised in an organisation that aims to understand collective processes.

Six authors joined together to create a mosaic of experiences linked to the development of Group Relations in China. Jeffrey Roth, Xiaohua Lu, Xumei Wang, Nick Bartlett, and Yu-Kuang Kevin Hsu review their various experiences from different roles over the years and conferences, which together create a very personal view of GR China. This creates a developmental perspective, which is then collected and organised by Seth Harkins, to give a conceptualisation of the developmental process of Group Relations in China in the years 2014–2021.

The chapter on "The Italian position", written by Claudio Cassardo with eight Italian colleagues, is based on work done by the 14 Italian participants in the conference, while it was taking place as well as in online meetings after it. In this sense it is a reflective chapter, but which we chose to place in this section, as it is an important contribution to the understanding of international and cultural perspectives on Group Relations. The chapter opens with the question of the existence of a specific Italian identity within Group Relations and continues to grapple with this question through the personal experiences and reflections of the authors. In this sense, it continues the method of the previous chapter, in that the authors offer

DOI: 10.4324/9781003502050-2

us personal "selfies" through which they reflect on cultural and national aspects of the Belgirate conference. Various vertices are used to highlight silenced aspects of the conference, such as the concrete silence of the Italian participants, power relations within the conference that were not spoken of, and the mind–body aspect of participating in an online conference. One such issue is what the authors call "the war of languages, the war of English, the overwhelming dictator". This came up in the editing of the chapter, which initially felt like a very direct translation of Italian into English. How much of this should be edited without being "overwhelmingly dictatorial"? The result is a compromise, with the aim of allowing non-Italians easier reading, while attempting to reduce the silencing of the Italian flavour of the chapter.

'For now we see through a glass, darkly ...': What PCCA means for the global Group Relations community and how Group Relations is in the heart of PCCA's work

Dorothee von Tippelskirch-Eissing

Introduction: Approaching the selfie

When I was invited in December 2019 to give a presentation at the 7th Belgirate conference the title sounded exciting to me, and then it changed its meaning quite a bit during the last two years of COVID-19.

What immediately came into my mind thinking about the 'Selfie' was not a psychoanalytic insight, not a moment of my Group Relations (GR) experiences, but a quote from the New Testament, quite important in Protestant theology, from a letter of Paul (1. Cor 13):

> When I was a child, I spoke as a child, I understood as a child, I thought as a child; but when I became a man, I put away childish things.
>
> For now we see through a glass, darkly but then face to face. Now I know in part; but then shall I know even as also I am known.

Thus, the title evoked immediately my different identity parts, being a Christian theologian and a psychologist, working as a psychoanalyst and now having been involved in GR for many years. As if I looked into a mirror.

I'll try to take you on a kind of journey between psychoanalysis and Protestant theology. And while I am speaking to you, I shall share with you three pictures of bowls, each broken and treated with the traditional Japanese art of repairing what is broken, in order to keep the container in function. The method is called Kintsugi. The bowls date from the sixteenth and seventeenth centuries.

The quote mentions looking at oneself in a mirror as an adult who has been a child, seeing but in part, *fragments*, but moving on towards a future of a specific face to face meeting, and hoping that from this face to face with the Other/God will come a kind of knowledge of oneself – a knowledge impossible to reach without this Other and a kind of movement between this Other and oneself.

DOI: 10.4324/9781003502050-3

Here you have already a kind of leitmotiv of PCCA's work: the work that needs to be done in the presence of the other.

Obviously, the element, "look into the mirror" reminds us as well of Narcissus, looking at himself. The deadly end of this story might remind us of stories about people taking selfies who suffer a terrible death in not paying attention to the reality around them – and falling into an abyss.

Selfies seem to be linked to a narcissistic position. We might be reminded of Freud, speaking about the three paths to destruction of the narcissistic illusion, the insult towards the love of oneself of human mankind: the cosmological insult by Copernicus, the biological by Darwin, and finally the psychological by Freud himself: the disappointment through the psychoanalytic discovery "that the Ego is not the master in his own house",[1] the subject thus being not free in a self-conscious dominating position, but a "sub-iectum" – I'd like to say: the one not without the other.

The biblical quote speaks about the limited and fragmented knowledge about ourselves, introducing a double problem: we look into a mirror with its specific torsions (like displacement and condensation, and yet, there is something different, something remaining in the dark, another quality of invisibility and limitation to knowledge. In theological language: something waiting to be revealed in the future, face to face, never present. This figure of the other remains the absolute condition for the possibility of whatever we might get to know about ourselves.[2] I will add another biblical association to the "Selfie" as an image of oneself, as a way of approaching the dark, the enigma: in one of the two biblical stories of creation the text speaks about the creation of the human being. The text says: "So God created man in his own image, in the image of God created he him; male and female created he them" (Gen 2, 27). There is this enigma of singular and plural, of two different sexes, in the image of the creator, obviously this image cannot be represented just by a single human "being". As the philosopher Emmanuel Lévinas might say: it is not in the being, but in the relation, the relation where the subject receives – following Lévinas – the command not to murder the other in the encounter with the face of the other, and where the primary task of the subject is to accept the responsibility for this other, the other that he has not chosen to be in relation with, but who has priority exactly in this way of confronting us and thus making us responsible. This basic relation could be one way to express the enigma, the hidden and unreachable image in the presence.

The selfie obviously comes along with the disappointment, the narcissistic wound. It might give testimony of our longing for something grandiose, pictures of us in front of a famous piece of architecture or nature – of the wish to appear in an idealised beauty. And, at the same time, these selfie-moments might talk about a deep lack of security, the fear of losing memory, of having passed by without making an impression, without leaving a trace.

Some of us might think of Lacan and the scene he has described of the baby recognising itself in a mirror for the first time, carried on mother's arm, and seeing itself in an upright position, which is not yet reachable for the baby by itself. Lacan has spoken of the reaction *jubilatoire* of the baby in this scene. At the centre of Lacan's interpretation there is the relationship between the carried baby, fragmented, not yet having the capacity to hold itself upright, and the carrying mother – and the interplay with the mirror.

There seems to be a part of this celebration – something we are longing for – and yet, there is limitation, fragmentation, distortion – the fragments, the pain, the despair, the vulnerability, the passivity, the end of knowledge and of capability.

I have mentioned the change in the meaning of the title of the conference over time since 2019.

I do think that GR knows a lot about the momentary, about partiality, something passing by, "the temporary institution", allowing a momentary view that will change, and should be changing, during the next moment. But the COVID-19 pandemic has changed some of the elements we are used to working with in an unexpected way.

New questions arose: would we be able to meet? Would it be safe? When? Where? Slowly, we began to have more and more meetings on Zoom, just like we are "meeting" today – faced constantly with our "selfies", seeing ourselves among others in a way we never did before, and yet, do we see each other? Can we address each other?

A third paper on the work of PCCA at Belgirate

Today, in PCCA, we can look back on a history of 13 conferences since 1994. I shall give you a list of these conferences in a moment.

In Belgirate there have been two presentations of PCCA, one in 2008, by Louisa Brunner, Fakhry Davids and myself, and the second by Shmuel Erlich in 2018.[3] Looking back at the moments of the presentations in Belgirate, it came to my mind that the interest PCCA has evoked in the GR world marked each time a specific moment in PCCA's life.

The first presentation in 2009 was given after the first six conferences and a shift of our focus, including not just Germans and Israelis and "affected others" but naming for the first time specific "Others" in the title of the conference, the Palestinians.

Here is a list of the first six PCCA conferences (1994–2008)

Three in Israel and Germany (1994–2000) Director: Eric Miller
Germans and Israelis: The Past in The Present
Three in Cyprus (2004–2010) Director: Anton Obholzer (2004–2008)
Germans, Jews and Affected Others: Shaping the Future by Confronting the Past (2004, 2006)
Germans, Jews, Palestinians & Others Today: Repeating, Reflecting Moving On (2008)

Thus, with the naming of the Palestinians, the aim of PCCA was enlarged from the "effects of the Holocaust" to "past and present national and international conflicts".

I think this move announced something that we only recently came to discuss in PCCA: the de-centralisation of the Holocaust in the work of PCCA.

After the following five conferences Shmuel gave his paper in Belgirate in 2018.

The list of the following five conferences, prior to Shmuel's paper (2010–2018):

One in Cyprus (2010) Co-Directors: Mira Erlich-Ginor and Fakhry Davids
"Germans, Jews, Palestinians & Others Today: Repeating, Reflecting Moving On"
Three in Poland (2012–2016) Director: Shmuel Erlich
"European Perpetrators and Victims – Now and Then" (2012)
"European Perpetrators and Victims – Then and Now" (2014)
"A House Divided Against Itself? Identities and Cultures in Violent Conflict" (2016)
And one in the Netherlands (2018) Director: Louisa D. Brunner
"Exclusion, Resentment and the Return of the Repressed: Europe in a Globalized World"

And, again there had been several changes: from Cyprus to Kliczkow (Poland) and to Den Dolder (Netherlands). The conference in 2010, with the same focus, including the Palestinians as specifically invited members, this time under the co-directorship of two PCCA members (Mira Erlich-Ginor, one of the founders of PCCA, and Fakhry Davids, belonging to the second generation among PCCA members) marked a specific date: a traumatic crisis for PCCA. In the aftermath, one might think about the specific process of transgenerational transmittal of trauma in the directorship.

I think the crisis from the conference in 2010 allowed us to move from Cyprus to Poland; the focus changed to a more European perspective. I understand this move as a compromise in the psychoanalytic sense of the term: it was a flight and a possibility for further development at the same time, again in the direction of decentralising the Holocaust in our work.

When we talked about this movement only a while ago, we could agree that the holocaust doesn't need to be in the centre, but we do think it belongs to the DNA of PCCA.

Between the last presentation of our work through Shmuel Erlich in 2018 and today, only three years have passed. And again, I think it is another specifically marked moment in the life of PCCA.

Looking at the conferences, during these three years we have had:

one "anniversary conference" in 2019, in Cyprus, Director: Mira Erlich-Ginor, explicitly mentioned as a "last conference of this kind": "80 Years later: Will History Repeat Itself? The Fallout of the Holocaust Over Those Affected. Looking Back, Moving Forward"

an online event in 2020, spontaneously reacting to the COVID-19 crisis, understood as another collective trauma, directed by Mira Erlich-Ginor: PCCA Virtual Event in the time of COVID-19. "Living. Experiencing, Reflecting in the Midst of Unfolding Global Turmoil" and our this year's PCCA-conference (2021), online, the conference postponed from 2020. Louisa, who has directed it, has talked about it in our meeting (see Chapter 5, this volume), "Walls – Open, Closed, Sliding? The Virus, Europe and our World Today"

Maybe it is worth noting, that two female colleagues from the first and second generation of PCCA members undertook the adventure of trying out a completely new format: a virtual one.

And something else happened during this period, one major event important to PCCA and we also think of the global GR world: PCCA received the Sigourney Award in 2019 – the most prestigious award in the world of psychoanalysis, an extraordinary acknowledgement of this project, the pain and care with which it has been born and raised since 1994.

We think that the attention PCCA has thus gained in the psychoanalytic world truly is a gain, which we owe to our common efforts: bringing together psychoanalytic insights and the thinking and the methodology of GR work in the application.

PCCA as part of the global Group Relations community – and Group Relations work inside PCCA

One of the distinguishing features of PCCA conferences lies in the history of the conferences: the project was designed from the outset to adapt GR methodology to its very specific purpose and membership,[4] which for many years involved psychoanalysts and psychotherapists in the "need to access and address the inner legacy of the Holocaust, which Israeli and German analysts (and others) recognized as being alive within them".[5] Among our sponsors of the project have been organisations such as OFEK and the Tavistock Institute, and especially three Psychoanalytic Societies, one from Israel (IPS) and two from Germany (DPV and DPG), recently also from Poland and the Netherlands, and our European Psychoanalytic Federation and International Psychoanalytic Association.

PCCA and the global Group Relations community: Collective trauma

I want to take up some ideas that Shmuel Erlich put forward in his paper at Belgirate three years ago, because I think this can well be a starting point for my own thoughts.

In his paper: "Unbounded worlds – A challenge for group relations?" he spoke to the historical background of the coming into being and evolving of GR in the 1950s (2018, p. 2). The hypothesis Shmuel gave, looking at the roots and the journey GR has taken, is that something happened which I would call a "compromise": GR dealt with this traumatic background of its own existence – the Second World War – by using the necessary defence in order to be able to work. Shmuel claims, "that the early phases of GR have unconsciously avoided the traumas that affected and burdened the world in which they were conceived" (2018, p. 6). In this sense he interpreted the traditional focus in GR as a defence against addressing or opening a space for "painful feelings", against dealing with the unbearable pain.

PCCA has taken up exactly this task, in addressing – in a very specific context – the residual effects and aftermath of the holocaust (p. 8), thus the meaning of PCCA for the GR world.

Shmuel had also given a reason for the necessity for applying GR methodology and thinking in approaching this space:

> The trauma, pain and suffering are at one and the same time the individual's and the group's, and the individual is affected *because of his "groupishness"*, as Bion put it, and therefore it can best be dealt with at the group level.
>
> (2018, p. 15)

He proposed a kind of "two parallel, equally important tracks" (p. 15): one track preserving the initial aims of GR and another track of "GRCs in which the learning and experiences gained in the first track are brought to bear on a variety of current and / or historical issues, where individual issues are contingent upon group identity, historical struggle and aspirations". Thus, GR is necessarily at the heart of PCCAs' work.

The German case

Thinking about my paper, I thought I might best speak to the experiential part of the German members in our conferences, even if this will be a very limited perspective, another fragment.

In German society there have been different phases in acknowledging that the atrocities committed during the years 1933–1945, and specifically since 1939, after the invasion of Poland, and 1942, the decision of the "final solution" and the deportation of the Jewish population and the murder of Jews and Jewish communities in Germany and Europe, is part of our history. To acknowledge, as Hanna Ahrendt had put it: "dass es so und nicht anders gewesen ist" – *that it has been what it has been and nothing else* – describes our history in Germany after the war.

The German historian, Jörn Rüsen has described the path in the following way: first – in the second generation – a strategy of "concealing knowledge" and "extra-territorializing", followed by "moral distancing" from the parents' generation. Through dissociation from National Socialism and counter-identification, this second generation developed an illusory deep sense of unity with the victims. And a third era, approximately at the time of the German reunification in 1989, with signs of a "historization and acknowledgement" of the Holocaust as the beginning of a German integration of identity: "We were the perpetrators".[6]

The project of the Nazareth Conferences started at this moment, in a time when there was a readiness and a need to work on such issues.

The beginning of this integration of the "perpetrator" into German identity had become the condition for the possibility of mourning.

Hermann Beland has named the content of this mourning as "the loss of the own 'Gutsein'" – our own *being good*.[7]

Beland has differentiated between three aspects of this mourning of the loss of our own good identity: first, the loss of our own humanity facing other nations as a humanity lost in murderous crimes, the second aspect touches on the questions of the historic grounds leading to delusional paranoid antisemitism, that is to understand the history of a collective mentality, and third: the acknowledgement and insight into a collective psychotic mentality effective in organising, realising and tolerating annihilating antisemitism.[8] This third aspect of the "psychotic mentality" seems to me to be one of the most important insights from the conference experiences for the German part.

Hermann gained this insight from his work with a small study group (SSG) in the fourth Nazareth conference. He got an answer to his question, why would Jewish/Israeli members take part in these conferences, when a member had said to him: "I want to meet your horror." He described at the same time his wish not to experience the murderous paranoia as his own, but he accepted the necessity to understand it from the inside, internally.

This problem is that of a psychotic breakdown beyond the individual, the domination of a destructive narcissistic organisation over the German people. Herbert Rosenfeld had attended a conference of our German Psychoanalytic Association (DPV) in 1984, which turned out to be one of the most important conferences on our path as psychoanalysts to deal with our collective position.

Rosenfeld (1984) said:

> If a psychotic powerful structure overcomes (*überwältigt*) a whole nation, it is extremely difficult to acknowledge the madness (*Verrücktheit*) entirely. Maybe it is only now that it is possible to study the deeper psychological elements that have overcome (*überwältigt*) the German Nation more than fifty years ago. I am afraid that the complete healing from this dangerous disease will take a very long time and will need active support.[9]

Concerning the collective genesis of this destructive narcissistic position, Beland reminds us of a description by Bion in *Transformations* (1965) of the existence of an absolute cruel power in analogy to existing objects, thus describing the horror of the Hitler mentality as group mentality:

> It is violent, greedy and envious, unscrupulous, murderous and rapacious, without respect for truth, people or things. It is what Pirandello might have called a character in search for an author. Having found a 'character' it seems to be a completely immoral conscience.[10]

I do think that what Rosenfeld has called an active support needed to heal from this dangerous disease, is exactly what GR work in PCCA conferences has meant for the German members. PCCA has brought Germans into conferences where they could gain insights of this kind into the collective madness and psychotic functioning while working in the "presence of the other".

I also want to add that there has been a place for possible hope. I remember having been in an SSG with an Israeli consultant. One of the German female members talked about a hereditary disease in her family, the pain was intense, and the atmosphere in the group was one of deep hopelessness. Until the Israeli consultant gave an interpretation: the group was fearing that the burden and pain in the aftermath of the Holocaust would be as unchangeable and endlessly repeated as a genetic constitution. This interpretation linking the most intimate individual destiny with the collective experience in the group, creating thus a language for the unbearable pain in the group had a powerful liberating effect, the atmosphere changed.

I think there are two perspectives where the power of this madness can be encountered, one seems to me to happen more inside German society and the other if Germans take part in an international discourse, as happened in this meeting.

Here is an example, from outside the conferences, but it could be part of a kind of "Review and Application" reflection:

Some time ago, we had a meeting of several colleagues, mostly training analysts of the Psychoanalytic Association to which I belong. We began to speak about our experience of this process of becoming a training analyst. We found out: each one of us could speak about either an accident, or a fall, a disease, a kind of intense pain during the process of becoming a training analyst, exactly at the moment when we were presenting our material to colleagues in our institutes or psychoanalytic society. In my view, it became obvious that what we had thought was an individual reaction, a somatic symptom in the context of an evaluation, a developmental move, turned out to be a symptom belonging to the group. In the aftermath of that meeting, I thought that in presenting our clinical papers, we were probably identified with a massively projecting object (S. Kitlitschko), our parents/our analytic parents, having transmitted this "dangerous disease" to us that Rosenfeld had mentioned. It is at the same time, of course, highly individual, formed by the collective mentality of Nazi Germany. I think it is the fear of complete annihilation of any movement/development, the fear of total exclusion and punishment, for any presentation of our own ideas. It belongs to the madness that is so difficult to be aware of, to acknowledge and to move on.

I also want to mention the other perspective, moving outside the German Society. Again, it has been Beland who has drawn attention to this point, how difficult, sometimes impossible, it is for German psychoanalysts taking up Freud's heritage to speak freely and contribute to the work in an international context. He has spoken of a "typical German, paranoid complex of guilt" as a legacy of the Holocaust. Again, in writing this paper, I have encountered this madness, the guilt and destructive loadings in a very intense way: again and again I had to fight the feeling that there is nothing I could possibly contribute and say to you. I realised that I don't just deal with the difficulty of writing about a complex issue, but that all kinds of forces seem to be mobilised to keep away from these traumatic issues, not to face them once again, and if so, the prize is to encounter not the usual doubts but in the depths the fear of annihilation, nameless anxiety and madness.

I'd like to finish with some remarks on the organisation, on PCCA, in order to refer once more to the question of the selfie:

We have moved on. I mentioned some of the changes: enlarging the perspective, opening up towards affected Others, Palestinians, Europeans. This year the conference had to be a virtual one. But even then, the metaphors that came up in the Social Dreaming Matrix (SDM) – the moment where the collective became the most visible maybe in this conference – in the midst of the global trauma of the COVID-19 pandemic emerged traces of the "traditional" PCCA German-Jews/Israeli themes. The question was posed whether this might have served as a defence – or is it still the reverberation of the "trauma and shame in Europe that deeply influences and impacts our lives?" (L. D. Brunner in her director's report.)

In my mind we need to keep this question open.

In an organisation that has chosen as its primary task to invite others to become partners in confronting collective atrocities, we have experienced that this means that some of the difficulties you expect in an organisation get filled with a very specific load: conflicts between members suddenly turn into extremely painful interactions, the depth of the traumatic ground that we share easily is touched.

It has been important to work with consultancy in order to free ourselves again and again from the projections, introjections, projective identifications that have a tendency to get personalised as well within an organisation that has the aim of understanding collective processes. We experience that this is helpful, especially in order to continue to move on towards an unknown future.

We have begun to invite new and younger colleagues to join, representing a new kind of diversity, also in the sense of our professions. As we developed initially from cooperation among psychoanalysts, there have mostly been psychoanalysts on the board of PCCA. Among the three new board members, Christoph Freytag, Oren Kaplan and Nadine Tchelebi, none of them is a psychoanalyst. We will be facing many questions concerning what this represents for our work and within our organisation.

Talking about a selfie of "partners in confronting collective atrocities", seems to speak about a picture that can be shaken into pieces/fragmented at any moment, whenever the traumatic content is touched; it seems to speak about the vigilance and the tolerance of those who are involved in this kind of encounter with the other, and about the pain that might result from this encounter, in order to do the necessary work to move on in the communities from which we come.

Doing the work in the presence of the other remains the central concept of the way in which we work and when we speak of collective mourning; we have found out that mourning in the presence of the other means that each group has to do this mourning separately, knowing the other is "next door".

Given the latest atrocity of COVID-19 and the global need to mourn terrible losses, it would seem that the work of PCCA and of group relations has never been so relevant as it is today.

In the beginning I presented to you the pictures of three broken and repaired ceramics, I shall end with another picture, showing to you a part of a memorial:

the picture shows the ground near one of the central churches in Berlin, the Kaiser Wilhelm Gedächtnis Kirche, partly ruined since the Second World War, a memorial in itself, and where, in 2016, the terror attack on the Christmas market took place – killing 13 people from Israel, Italy, Ukraine, Poland, the Czech Republic and Germany, and leaving many seriously wounded. It is a golden crack in the ground.

Notes

1 S. Freud, in "Eine Schwierigkeit in der Psychoanalyse", *GW*, 12, S. 3–12.

2 I'd like to remind us of the title of the Festschrift that Mira Erlich-Ginor has composed for Shmuel Erlich: *Not knowing – Knowing – Not Knowing*: *Festschrift Celebrating the Life and Work of Shmuel Erlich*, (IPbooks, 2017), and to which some of us present here have contributed. Mira writes in the Introduction, concerning her choice: "Shmuel assumes that all is transient and at most, partly known. He sees the quest for 'knowing' as an illusion, and 'not-knowing' not as a lack but as an important existential state" (p. xvi). Both of them, Mira and Shmuel, have been important teachers to me in the world of GR, and it is also a way to express my gratitude for the invitation to speak to you today, trying to do my best in following Shmuel, who spoke about our work in PCCA here – in Belgirate – three years ago.

3 "Germans, Jews, Israelis, Palestinians and Others today: Thoughts on the 'Nazareth' conferences" in Belgirate III in Nov 2009, by the author together with Louisa D. Brunner and M. Fakhry Davids, and "Unbounded Worlds – A Challenge for Group Relations?" In Belgirate VI in 2018, by Shmuel Erlich.

4 A detailed report on the design of the first conferences can be found in the book on the first three Nazareth conferences: *Fed with Tears – Poisoned with Milk. The 'Nazareth' Group-Relations-Conferences: Germans and Israelis: the Past in the Present*, with a Preface by Archbishop Desmond M. Tutu, Hermann Beland, Mira Erlich-Ginor and Shmuel Erlich (Eds), Psychosozial Verlag, Gießen, 2009, pp. 35–47.

5 Louisa D. Brunner, M. Fakhry Davids, and Dorothee C. von Tippelskirch-Eissing, "Germans, Jews, Israelis, Palestinians, and Others today: thoughts on the 'Nazareth' conferences", in: *Group Relations Conferences. Tradition, Creativity, and Succession in the Global Group Relations Network*, Vol III, Eliat Aram, Robert Baxter, and Avi Nutkevitch (Eds), Karnac, 2012, p. 69.

6 H. Beland, "The stages of the German psychoanalysts on their way to the First Nazareth Conference", in: *Fed with Tears – Poisoned with Milk. The 'Nazareth' Group-Relations-Conferences: Germans and Israelis: the Past in the Present"* (2009), p. 21.

7 H. Beland, "Kollektive Trauer. Wer oder was befreit ein Kollektiv zu seiner Trauer?" ["Collective mourning. Who or what liberates a collective to its mourning" (transl. DvTE); in: H.B. Unaushaltbarkeit. *Psychoanalytische Aufsätze II zu Theorie, Klinik und Gesellschaft*, Gießen, 2011, pp. 449–468, p. 456ff.

8 H. Beland, "Kollektive Trauer. Wer oder was befreit ein Kollektiv zu seiner Trauer?" ["Collective mourning. Who or what liberates a collective to its mourning" (transl. DvTE); in: H.B. Unaushaltbarkeit. *Psychoanalytische Aufsätze II zu Theorie, Klinik und Gesellschaft*, Gießen, 2011, p. 457.

9 H. Rosenfeld (1984), quoted by H. Beland in, "Kollektive Trauer. Wer oder was befreit ein Kollektiv zu seiner Trauer?" ["Collective mourning. Who or what liberates a collective to its mourning" (transl. DvTE); in: H.B. Unaushaltbarkeit. *Psychoanalytische Aufsätze II zu Theorie, Klinik und Gesellschaft*, Gießen, 2011, p. 467.

10 W.R. Bion, *Transformations*, 1965, p. 146; quoted by H. Beland in, "Kollektive Trauer. Wer oder was befreit ein Kollektiv zu seiner Trauer?" ["Collective mourning. Who or what liberates a collective to its mourning" (transl. DvTE); in: H.B. Unaushaltbarkeit. *Psychoanalytische Aufsätze II zu Theorie, Klinik und Gesellschaft*, Gießen, 2011, p. 468.

2

Group Relations in China

Portraits (selfies) of cross-cultural trust and organisational development 2014–2021

Seth Harkins, Nicholas Bartlett, Yu-Kuang Kevin Hsu, Xiaohua Lu, Jeffrey D. Roth, and Xumei Wang

This chapter provides a longitudinal perspective of group relations in China from 2014 to 2021 through portraits or selfies of our experience in group relations. We use a theory of trust to organise our experiences in various roles and reveal eight stages of group relations development, which will be discussed in the implications section of this chapter. Our theory of trust is drawn from Lewicki and Bunker (1995) who posit three stages of trust. Our eight stages of organisational development were influenced by Burke (2018).

The Director's Selfie, Jeffrey D. Roth, MD

My role began with taking up my personal and professional authority to initiate the Beijing Group Relations Conference (BGRC) 2014: "Authority and Leadership in Recovery from Mental Illness and Addiction" and three subsequent GRCs in 2016 and 2018. The inspiration for exporting this to China was from Huzeyin Ozdemir's (2015) keynote presentation at the Belgirate conference in 2012 on the GRCs that he directed between 2010 and 2012 in Wuxi, China. Having received a grant to conduct a GRC with the theme of authority and leadership in recovery from mental illness and addiction at the University of Chicago Beijing Center (UCBC), I began a complicated and complex cross-cultural venture. I had no formalised professional network in China. I did not have any institutional affiliations with Chinese organisations, except the University of Chicago.

Using my psychiatry and group psychotherapy networks, I recruited a directorate including both Western and Chinese staff. These team members representing the UCBC and the Division of Group Counselling and Group Therapy (DGCGT) of the Chinese Association for Mental Health (CAMH) joined to launch the enterprise. The initiative could not have succeeded without the assistance of Tsinghua University Professor Fumin Fan. A leading scholar in group psychotherapy and the chairperson of the DGCGT, she was invaluable in developing the infrastructure for the 2014 BGRC. She and her associate, Xiaohua Lu, broadcast the idea of a GRC to thousands of Chinese mental health and addiction professionals, resulting in a membership of 60 with a waiting list.

DOI: 10.4324/9781003502050-4

My authorisation emanated from five sources. First, the consulting staff from the US had worked with me in conferences that I had directed in Chicago. These US consultants were available to receive a host of feelings and projections from our Chinese hosts about foreigners from countries with colonising histories.

A second source was a bilingual staff. He/she who has control of the language has authority, power, and cultural hegemony. Rather than using exact language translation, which I believed imposed a barrier to consultation in the here-and-now, a team of cultural interpreters (CIs) was created. Their task was to synthesise here-and-now experiences and share them in English with consultants as data for consultations. With this data, consultants formulated interpretations of group phenomenon in small study groups (SSGs), large study groups (LSGs), review and application groups (RAGs), and institutional event (IE) groups. The CIs served as cultural bridges between Mandarin and English-speaking staff. By the time we launched the 2017 Beijing SSG Conference, the 2018 Beijing residential conference, and the 2019 Shanghai LSG Training Conference, CIs transitioned to consultants-in-training. Cultural interpretation emerged organically with English and Chinese seeking language interpretation from each other or group members. Importantly, taking up authority to speak in English involved vulnerability and risk on the part of Mandarin speakers, who were sometimes being seen as disloyal and thus became the targets of projections.

Third, the working consultant–CI pair relationship represented another level of authorisation. The CIs were projection objects for detoured feelings about the consultants. They were convenient targets for feelings of hatred, anger, competition and envy. Considerable risk and vulnerability were apparent, as the CIs were perceived as "running dogs", a slur referring to the Chinese who supported colonial masters. In this context, consultant authority was crucial in interpreting displaced, covert feelings and dynamics of avoiding (de-authorising) or working with (authorising) consultants. Members adapted, authorising the consultants/CIs and themselves.

Fourth, experiential learning represented another source of authorisation. Top-down, teacher-to-student pedagogy has been the traditional model of teaching and learning in China. Members expected consultants to explicitly teach about GR and recovery from mental illness and addiction. When consultants took up a non-directive consultancy stance, group members expressed anger, hatred and disappointment.

Fifth, the membership constituted another source of authority. Given the historical–cultural realities of Western imperialism, members expressed suspicion of our motives in bringing GR and Twelve Step recovery to China. Was this some experiment in which the staff gathered its data and went off to analyse it and not return? These suspicions crystallised when members challenged me and the staff about whether the conference was a one-night stand or an invitation to exploring a partnership and committed relationship. If our Chinese colleagues shared an interest in developing a committed relationship, my availability was unambiguous. We returned in 2016 with the Hong Kong GRC (UCHKC) and 2016 BGRC, 2018 BGRC, 2019 Changsha GRC, and 2020 e-GRC.

Boundaries

Boundary crossing in this cross-cultural enterprise was an extraordinarily complex undertaking. The conferences held between 2014 and 2016 involved continued challenges regarding boundary crossing, navigation and management. These occurred on multiple levels: institutional, professional, logistical, linguistic and cultural. A non-Mandarin speaker, I was completely dependent upon my Chinese colleagues to facilitate recruitment, work with the UCBC and UCHKC administrators, and marketing across mainland China. China is by no means a homogenous culture, comprising highly diverse regional differences, identities and cultures. Traversing these boundaries required a complete leap of faith in trusting new relationships to move a vision to concrete reality.

I knew the importance of establishing "good enough" boundaries to hold and contain the disparate parts of the conference. With a clear holding environment, members are able to regress, allow the unconscious impulse in the group not only to come forth, but also examine such impulses as group-as-a-whole phenomena. In 2014 I learned firsthand the complexity of the task of boundary management and regulations. Establishing an atmosphere of respect and collaboration regarding language was essential, hence the creation of the CI cultural bridge.

A second learning about boundaries involved staffing for the 2016 HKGRC and 2016 BGRC. As a director sponsoring a new technology in China, I wanted an international staff capable of providing excellent consultation. I also wanted a staff that would push me to be as skilful and expert a director as I could be. I invited a group of international consultants that included a British consultant with Jamaican heritage, two Australians and an Israeli. I invited not only gifted consultants but also critics with the ability to interrogate my/our work.

Training and working with one another across linguistic and cultural boundaries provided a third significant learning about boundaries. Each conference was preceded by two days of staff meetings. In simulated SSGs, Chinese staff worked member roles, while consultant–CI pairs practised taking up consultant and CI roles. In each of these experiences, splitting, projection, projective identification and basic assumption groups emerged, becoming rich data for staff learning. What I learned was the importance of working with risk, vulnerability, and trust prior to the conference opening.

Role

In taking up my role and role authority, I was able to examine my directing and leadership style. Over the years I came to see hierarchies embedded in relationship networks and webs. I also came to see effective directing as a collaborative process of authorising and trusting. This meant involving the staff in the decision-making about issues that would affect our collective work. In the 2014 and 2016 GRCs, my efforts at collaboration were met with complaints about my leadership not being "hard edged". For some, I was not being "authoritative" in terms of decision making. Some staff perceived me as blurring the boundaries between the director and staff roles and tasks. I was further seen as unprepared and unanticipating of events. What I saw as an invitation to collaboration and enquiry, others perceived as "twelve steppy". I used "group conscience" as symbolic of group consensus decision making. Some regarded it as "not group relations". The criticism was that my style was a social defence against what was occurring within the staff-as-a-whole. The wish for an authoritative, or authoritarian, director competed with my attempts at collaboration.

What was clear by the conclusion of the 2016 BGRC was that conference dynamics were extremely complex. This complexity was influenced by several factors. First, the HKGRC and BCRC were conducted back-to-back. Second, the diversity of the staff challenged our ability to form a cohesive work group. The returning staff from 2014 BCGRC had worked with me on several dual track conferences. The new international staff did not have this experience and questioned the efficacy of integrating two group different models of relating to others in groups. A third factor was my willingness to hear and learn from criticism. A post-conference debriefing suggested the dual track model was too complex and too difficult to hold to make room for interpretative work. It was suggested that I be more of a CEO role in planning the conferences and delegating more authority to others. A single-track conference was recommended for 2018. Envisioning a future all-Mandarin speaking conference, I accepted this recommendation. In the 2017 Beijing SSG Conference and the 2019 Shanghai LSG conference, I took on the CEO role, hiring directors.

The critiques were important in my role in 2018 BGRC. As a single-track residential conference, opportunities for staff and member processing were optimised with expanded time. I was also keenly aware of my need to take on the projections of anger and rage within the staff. This leadership task appeared when the detoured staff projections were located on a co-consultant, who, without my intervention, may have become the staff scapegoat and conference casualty. I was direct and clear that I "wanted the anger". Holding the complex staff parts was evident in a staff conversation about Tiananmen Square. I recognised powerful projections at play -- the conference was held during the anniversary of the Square protest.

Task

I have seen my role as facilitating an organisational infrastructure. This infrastructure has included building partnerships, recruiting talented foreign and Chinese staff, and training future Chinese GRC practitioners. None of this would have been possible without delegating authority and responsibility to others. Central to all of this has been negotiating trust across a wide range of historical, cultural, and linguistic boundaries. Learning from my/our successes and challenges, the task going forward is to continue the GR work and realise the vision of GRCs in China, which will be GRC with Chinese characteristics, appreciating the collectivism inherent in Chinese history and culture. The 2019 Changsha conference represented an important transition point. The conference was conducted predominantly in Mandarin and Chinese co-consultants paired with experienced American and Western consultants. The task in Changsha was complicated by intense competition, envy, and ambition in two powerful women, both of whom wished to be the first Chinese director of a Chinese GRC. The themes of conflict and trust were imported into e-GRC China 2020, the first online GRC in China. The task in this conference was to extend the transition in language and personnel, as this conference was conducted entirely in Mandarin. Issues of trust and conflict were amplified with the addition of a research team, which observed and documented staff work across the four-day conference during the COVID-19 pandemic. The advent of the research team stimulated considerable anxiety and fear of evaluation and surveillance in the conference as well as society. The task was additionally complicated by a Directorate, LSG Team, SSG Team and Research Team, each of which had American, mainland Chinese, and Taiwanese representatives, reflecting the geopolitical relations of the mainland China, Taiwan, and America.

My roles and experience in Group Relations Conference in China 2014–2021, Xiaohua Lu, PhD

I am a psychologist, the secretary general of DGCGT,CMHA, a co-founder of CASSGO. I participated in the GRC programme since 2014 when Jeffrey Roth reached out to me through Winnie Fei. I connected Jeffrey Roth and Fumin Fan together to begin a partnership with DGCGT and the CMHA.

2014: Trust in Chaos

In 2014, Winnie Fei approached me and asked if I would like to win the support of Professor Fan to support a man named Jeffrey in a group relations conference in China. I asked her whether this group conference was the group relations conference that Ruthellen Josselson wanted to promote in China. Winnie said yes. So, I said, "Yes."

Jeffrey secured a grant from the University of Chicago to fund this and cooperated with DGCGT,CMHA to hold a GRC at the UCBC. We accepted 60 people out of 80 applicants. Since the core pre-conference staff come from the USA and China we were strangers cooperating through the Internet. We were full of anxiety and uncertainty.

There were lots of authority issues during 2014 Beijing GRC. I was the person authorised by Fumin Fan to cooperate with Jeffrey. I worked under Jeffrey's direction. Winnie represented Jeffrey, which meant I worked under her direction. I had the responsibility of monitoring the programme to make sure that it would not negatively reflect the Chinese people as another "Eight-nation invasion". So, there were authority issues between the US and China, represented by Dr Roth and Professor Fan, through Winnie and me.

Also, there were authority issues between Winnie and Jeffrey about interpretation, whether to provide exact translation or culture interpretation (CI). Ultimately,

CI prevailed, and a cadre of cultural interpreters was recruited and trained to partner with Western consultants.

2016: Split and Resistance

As an administrator in 2016, I could sense plenty of challenges and conflicts during this conference. Staff complained about their accommodations. There was a lack of trust toward Jeffrey. I could not understand all these conflicts. I was very anxious about being "killed" in this conference. Tavistock, Australia GR, and OFEK were represented in the staff along with Americans. Also, a subgroup from Yalom Institute participated as members. Most of the international staff challenged the dual-track model of GRC and Jeffrey's authority. The entire staff felt divided. Yalom programme members challenged the director, objecting to GRC's consultation stance. They wished for direct responses, personal contact and warmth from the consultants. This subgroup came for the final SSG and then left the conference. I felt the fragmentation within me. After an evening meeting, I rode an electric scooter home. In order to avoid a pedestrian, I swerved, hit a tree and fell off the scooter. Fortunately, there was no major injury.

There was an attempt to repair the split. At the closing dinner, two women went to the Contemporary Mall and bought two silk scarves for ADA Mary Walker and me for our administrative work. One of the women represented AKRI and the other OFEK. Their gifts expressed condolences to the administrative team for the torture we suffered. As we know, the administrative team can easily become a scapegoat before and after the entire meeting.

2018 Beijing GRC: Dependent and Interdependent

I took the role of assistant director for administration in the 2018 BGRC. The CI was eliminated and replaced with Chinese co-consultants. Chinese and English consultants asked each other for cultural interpretations. English-speaking staff were dependent on Mandarin-speaking staff to understand here-and-now dynamics. Mandarin-speaking staff similarly depended on the English-speaking staff to consult. This language shift reflected a transition, with Mandarin becoming the more dominant language.

Two events stand out for me in this conference. First, a Chinese consultant, a Hong Kongese woman, challenged me, asking for equal treatment with foreign consultants. I was shocked at that time. I could not understand her. In China, I have been educated to give better food to the guest, be humble, this is the first time I learned that we can ask for equal rights, and respect ourselves. A second was a conversation about the conference being held during 4th June, which is a special date in China. I recall during one staff meeting at the end of the day, we Chinese talked about the trauma in our history. Our foreign consultants wanted to empathise, but an angry exchange occurred about the Tiananmen Square protest. I felt uncomfortable and in pain. I felt I didn't need foreigners to care for me. I felt anger toward them because some traumas were related to them. Foreign consultants felt being wronged, and they felt they wanted to understand but got badly treated. I sensed the different national identities and different national emotions.

The main dynamics of this conference were about being dependent and interdependent. Chinese consultants were maturing, finding their own voice, the power begin to shift to more Mandarin dominance but with some anxiety, hesitation and suspicion.

2019 Changsha GRC: Competition among Mainland Chinese consultants

I was a visiting scholar in the US in 2018–2019. I came back to China, going directly to Changsha for the 2019 GRC, an all-Mandarin conference. Foreign consultants communicated with non-verbal language. I was an SSG consultant, with my new identity as a co-founder of CASSGO, and still as the General Secretary of DGCGT, CAMH.

I had a very strong conflict with Xumei, ten years older, a psychiatrist and a professor. I am a Chinese Communist Party member. She is a different party member. I could sense her anger, distrust toward me, but I could not figure out the dynamics. I thought she envied me. I could sense a lot of competition among staff. One Chinese consultant came to me and told me that she would compete with me and surpass me in the future. My image for the CGRC is one of heroes, fights and terrible conflicts. It seems that we went from learning from and competing with foreign consultants to competition and conflict among ourselves. It was a painful conference. I remember I cried heavily alone in the bathroom at 3.00 a.m. Many Chinese staff were angry with me. I was just shocked and could not say anything.

2020 e-GRC: Trust and Distrust

The Changsha fight continued into the 2020 e-GRC. Another occurred regarding the research planned for the Shenyang GRC 2020. I had a strong fear that I would be "killed" if Xumei was the principal investigator for the research. The pandemic intervened and the Shenyang GRC evolved into e-GRC China. Jeffrey decided to put me into the research team instead of the consultant team, and Xumei became ADA, leaving the research to be directed by Seth Harkins and Kevin Hsu.

There were two incidents, a technology failure of the opening plenary and conflict regarding the mainland and Taiwan relationship. An angry Taiwanese shouted at me that I could not understand her; that I could not understand Taiwanese people. I felt wronged. We are family. Why so angry? The Taiwan–mainland, US dynamics in GRC in China emerged. I learned to be silent and just follow the dynamics. I noticed that things could go well when I do nothing. I know, I am not as important as I thought.

2021e-GRC: Envy, Competition and Collaboration

I was the director of this conference sponsored by CASSGO & DGCGT, CAMH. I directed a staff of 18 (eight men, 11 women.) Thirteen were older than me. In China, men have more authority than women. Elders have more than younger persons. The core staff dynamics of this conference strongly challenged my authority. Three persons were selected to challenge me. One was the LSG team head. The other was my associate director. The associate director was not my first choice; Jeffrey recommended her to be the associate with the hope of cultivating more collaboration between us. I agreed with Jeffrey after some time hesitation. The ADA was also recommended by Jeffrey. I agreed with this recommendation even though he had no GRC administrative experience. Another challenge was over the composition of LSG and SSG teams. The LSG team head insisted on changing the structure of four LSG consultants, which meant switching SSG consultants to the LSG. We asked Jeffrey to consult to this. He recommended authorising the two team heads to work it out between them.

Another challenge to me occurred when the associate director and the ADA wanted to change the structure of the IE just nine minutes before the IE. I firmly stopped this. Later, a conflict with them involved the distribution of digital room keys and consultation to the inter-group room. Despite the challenges to my authority, I survived. The first aeroplane piloted by Mandarin-speaking staff successfully landed.

From Member to Consultant to ADA to Associate Director, Xumei Wang, MD, PhD

I began my first GRC in Beijing 2016 with strong curiosity and suspicion. I had never heard of an experiential learning conference, even though I had participated in a lot of professional conferences in China and abroad as a psychiatrist. In the Opening Plenary I was very scared of director, who appeared very strict and cold, reminding me of my father. I felt warm and contained in my SSG group, but the consultant did not look at us and ended each session exactly on time without telling us! I felt powerful and stable when a member challenged the "big boss" by wanting him to move his seat. I also felt warm and learned about the importance of boundaries in the RAG. When I asked the consultant to take a photo with me, she refused. After the conference, my brain kept on reflecting for more than six months! I understood a lot about myself, my family and my professional relationships, applying it to my various back home lives. I really learned more about myself and felt more confident by learning from this experiential approach. Chinese education is teacher-centred, not learner-centred. I began trusting this approach, the director and staff. This trust and my passion inspired me to participate in the 2017 Beijing Small Study Group training and beyond. Since I trusted Jeffrey and foreign colleagues, I applied to the AKRI Training and Certification Committee for consultant candidacy, choosing Seth as my mentor.

In Chinese culture the individual must surrender to the collective. I have been a good follower since childhood. I knew the changes in me were real and profound when I took up my own authority in the Beijing 2018 GRC. I challenged the director by expressing my anger for twice changing my working partner without consulting me. I wanted to work with Seth with the transferences with my trauma in relation to my father and family history. I was eventually paired with Isabelle Reineger, an American consultant. There was tension and conflict in our co-consultancy. The working languages were Mandarin and English, but without cultural interpreters. When Isabelle asked me to translate for her, I wondered: was I a co-consultant or culture interpreter? Eventually I took up my authority and role as a consultant when I made my first consultation. I felt competition with Isabelle. I could understand Chinese She could not. I was envious of her experience and certification by AKRI. Besides that, we also had strong envy and competition between and among Chinese colleagues. Who is the best daughter of the director? Who spoke the best English?

My continuing passion for learning about person role and system and my trust in Jeffrey and Seth helped me to join the 2019 Changsha conference as an SSG consultant. In the context of China's thousands of years of history of envy, competition and trauma, Xiaohua, and I enacted our competition to be the first Chinese director of a GRC in the Changsha GRC in 2019. By strenuous fighting in staff meetings, we were consciously and unconsciously encouraged to fight by the staff. This allowed the silent staff to avoid its anger with the director and competition with each other.

In e-GRC China 2020, I took the role as ADA, a different role, different vantage point and organisational perspective. There were significant issues of conflict and trust evident in unspoken dual and multiple relationships. And there was competition for the favorite daughter status and intimacy with the director.

In the 2021 Wuhan GRC, I took up the role of associate director. Can I trust Xiaohua as a director and collaborate with her? Sometimes I did and sometimes I did not. My learning in this role involved continuing to take an interpretative consulting stance, promoting collaboration where I could. Xiaohua and I have our differences but also shared beliefs about the value of group relations to facilitate systems change. Xiaohua is an authority in CASSGO. She grew up in a CCP family which is respected very much by many Chinese. She is also an associate professor, and a psychologist. I grew up in a traumatised family. My grandparents were landlords and identified as the "enemy of the people". My grandparents were beaten to near death and committed suicide. We had very conflictual feelings about authority. Like Xiaohua, I am a mental health professional and university professor. The fight between us is about our competition, envy, ambition and shame. We fought because we mistrusted each other. Our competition is bigger than both of us. It is about how we struggle to trust and resolve conflicts without "killing" each other. It is about the possibility of resolving conflicts collaboratively through the use of group relations practices. We also share a commitment to applying our group relations learning to our personal and organisational lives. In Chinese culture it is often difficult to find clear relationship boundaries. Guanxi relationships involve many special relationships, which are the dominant influences in interpersonal, family, community, and professional endeavours.

Growing in the work in China, Nick Bartlett, PhD

My introduction to the group relations tradition took place through a fortunate coincidence. Trained as a medical anthropologist with previous experience living in China and coursework in psychoanalysis, I learned about group relations work from Jeffrey Roth, who reached out after my name came up in an internet search. He convinced me that participating in Tavistock tradition conferences in China would be a fascinating way for me to further my interests in the country's changing mental health landscape. Since 2018, I have attended several conferences in the US and China in member and staff roles.

The conferences for me have been spaces of intense learning that have provoked profound questions about collective life in China and the USA, as well as my own personal relationship to leadership and authority. In Beijing in 2018, my first conference in China, organisers had intentionally decided to not provide interpretation services for a bilingual conference. Attending as a member, my first attempt to translate in the LSG occurred an hour in on the first day. Numerous Chinese members applauded when I finished. A bilingual Chinese woman member angrily pointed out the discrepancy between the group's reaction to her numerous previous translations and those made by me, a white American male. Participating in this Beijing GRC magnified the privileges and dangers taken up by those assuming the translator role, while also highlighting longstanding language ideologies and assumptions about who should do what types of language-related work in the conferences.

A second memory comes from my own participation in a Chinese staff at a conference in Changsha, my fourth GRC and first time on staff as a "co-consultant". I was also acutely aware that my own GRC work in the region was beginning to deepen as other foreign consultants who had participated in previous meetings were preparing to leave as conferences moved towards being conducted exclusively in Mandarin. One evening, Taiwanese and mainland Chinese members gathered for an intimate and intense discussion, which I attended. Witnessing how this group experienced connection through resemblance and imagined kinship, I felt happiness for my colleagues, but at the same time a deep loneliness as I questioned my presence and role at the meeting, and at China conferences more generally. The conference provided a valuable opportunity to reflect on belonging and exclusion in these times of great tumult and tense geopolitical relations.

In the 2020 e-GRC, I served as an "observer" on the research team, which had trouble establishing trust with other parts of the staff. I was not authorised to speak in many meetings and had my camera off for most sessions. I was often unsure about when and how to offer feedback to other members of the staff. In attending sessions with members, I also became aware of how our presence also raised complicated feelings about authorisation and safety, in the process helping me to formulate new perspectives on who the research was for and how it should be conducted and transmitted.

I took part in the 2020 e-Wuhan GRC directed by Xiaohua Lu. Wondering about whether we were competent enough to "fly our own plane" was a key question for the staff as a whole. In this Mandarin only conference, at moments I struggled to stay in role as I faced both idealising and devaluing projections. More recently, I also participated in other related trainings and conferences in mainland China and Taiwan. While exciting, taking on different administrative and consulting roles has brought up new challenges, navigating not only the complicated relationship between the US, mainland China and Taiwan, but also different factions within the greater Chinese GRC community in a time of competition and growth.

Looking forward, I anticipate continuing to grapple with what I represent in this system. At times, I have been viewed with suspicion as a spy planted by Jeffrey and Seth, and others who specifically asked not to attend particular post-conference events due to my status as a foreigner. While some might see my presence as a continuation of the white American male authority in the conference, I have also at times struggled to navigate expectations as one of the more junior members on Chinese conference staffs. In future conferences, I am excited to continue to grow personally while participating in the rapid growth of tradition in the region in a time of great innovation and experimentation.

Standing on the bridge under the dense fog: Reviewing the multiple realities and tangled expectations through the corner, Yu-Kuang Kevin Hsu, PhD

Due to the difficulties of historical reality and context, the daily indirect exposure to the media's discussion of cross-strait relations, generally has influenced the mindset of Taiwan residents. Over the years, as a participant, trainee, consultant and research team leader, my GRC experience in mainland China from 2016 to the present has seemed to me an adventure which had the benefit of releasing the accompanying growth trajectory. In particular, "making up the puzzle" is a good metaphor to express the many moments of learning that turn into real connections, both from team experience and teamwork with colleagues and friends from different regions. To me, it seemed to fill in the gaps in those fractured historical contexts and understandings of mainland China that had been excluded from Taiwanese textbooks in the past, and it froze fantasies in my K-12 schooling.

The corner for standing

I take selfies on daily basis in my diary. I am reminded by a few photos from the GRC China experience when the subject was proposed at a conference in Belgium. Swimming in both idealisation and devaluation seems to be an extreme dynamic that is sometimes strongly present in the system. For example, female subgroups tend to show tenderness, attentiveness, enthusiasm, or self-restraint in the impression of Taiwanese men through soft accents, which are easily projected onto my image as a dependable professional. Also, there is the separation from male or female due to competitive attitudes, verbal aggression, or demeaning complex emotions such as anger, jealousy or unhappiness. It looks like a selfie, an ambiguous underground target with many sparks of war in the sky, and then sometimes two parts turn to you and ask for your opinion, forcing you to show the side you're on.

In my awareness, I named this kind feeling as "the Corner Standing" in the China GRC system. It presented between the issues such as gender, senior and junior, opposite opinions, also the staffs of Chinese and foreigners, and even the different attitudes toward Taiwan's historical realities. It seems this could be linking with my behaviour of withdrawal, passivity, and a little fear to take a role in the group or staff team, which prompts my reflection of a corner-style identity for me in the fight or conflict. From my experience, I explore the ways to connect, enter, or stand. It is a process of finding your voice as not hidden within yourself, which is figuring out your strength in the system and as a process of *inside-out* to find your voice. Conversely, the conflict resolution process also helped me to explore the positions, space or energy through the impacts on the interpersonal and within or between the groups' dimensions, which to me was trying to know who you have been, are, should be, could be and will be. These identities are a kind of *outside-in* process for updating the selfie, enhancing the possibility of leaving the corner and onward.

The multiple realities

The selfies' changes during the years attended also reflected the multiple realities. The Western psychology tradition has had a very strong influence on the society, for many scholars were sponsored by USA institutes in the late 20th century and studied abroad, then returned to Taiwan where this is called, through our introspection, *academic colonisation*. My first large group experience was enlightened by the instructor in 1994. It was in a group dynamic class of undergraduates and graduates. This was my starting point for learning. Also, it was a context for swinging between superiority (if I know something) or inferiority (if I don't know). The Eastern side, about the strong emotional bonding with mainland China, the land and people, who also are presented in a kind of psychological closeness or sibling feeling in some ways for connection through very specific interactions. It underlines as a back and forth between the interactions when the member recognised the Taiwanese sibling was here as a target, either friendly and warm, or sometimes confronting you very quickly but rarely showing the hatred.

These two strengths between Western and Eastern, the push–pull and invisible projections, was a dynamic in my joining experience. For example, it's easy to be close and familiar with new friends from the same culture as Chinese, but, for the reality of historic isolation, the vocabularies needed to be clarified or converted for correct understanding. Conversely, my higher educated background has been projected as a resource. Sometimes it looks as if I understand very well what the foreigner consultant said, even though sometimes actually I have no idea. What's the truth? Or what ways could I see the realities of the selfie "I" in the system? Although I encouraged myself to leave the corner, I'm still on the way, searching for my selfie.

As the bridge – on/at/in the middle

The tangled relationship brought a mirroring of the system represented as a triangulation dynamic which placed me both as the bridge and standing on it in some significant moments. For example, the *within but also between* positions showed on the occasions of translation, plus interpretation when I talked or discussed with both sides between the "we" and the "foreigner". It's not really necessary, but extrusion within the dynamic, and a kind feeling of care or connecting with both, is the position of standing at the middle. For example, the members used me to talk with the consultant, or the foreigner consultant, which proposed the confused question that may alter the "We" to me. Another example is the research team. The researchers cannot save digital files on the same shared drive because of the Internet wall. Thus, as the assistant director for research, I took up the role of information keeper. Research data is stored on two shared drives – one for Chinese and one for Americans. As a Taiwanese I can access both and make data exchanges. The bridge is a symbolic position of my selfie feelings, standing in the middle when I deal with the details and move all bricks from east to west then west to east.

The dense fog

The selfie seems covered by the dense fog, with hazy and beautiful scenery underneath but it needs to hide in the fog, sometimes lightly drifting or gathering suddenly, induced by a strong physical sensation or very strong emotions, on a specific member, staff, subgroup or team. The emotionality of the GRC system across several years had its own character or sensations, seemingly suffering some kind of painful or shameful voice on one side, and the feeling of uncertainty or fear of the separate if differences emerged on another side. The wishes to enhance the personal growth, carry forward the GRC model and promote societal development would be our tasks on the conscious level, while the expectation of learning together and genuinely connecting to each other being hindered and covered up by the dense fog. It still presents as difficult on the unconscious level for the future.

Moved from the corner or left the middle

In the 2020 China GRC, I took the role of assistant director for the research team and a member of the management team. This clear duty brought the moving and shifting for me in the system. It ran through my hidden years and evoked my learning under the sunshine, which include:

The boundaries. Trying to face the unknowns, accepting the intercrossing of boundaries were important learning for me on the ways to growth and creating new boundaries.

The authorities. It's a parallel process of losing my persistency trying to understand the hierarchy of power in the system.

The roles. Through the process of familiarity and acceptance, the roles opened for me to try a new one, such as consultant in training, consultant, and research team leader. I experimented with new roles.

The tasks. The comfortable area with fighting and rediscovering my voice, which was no longer silent, repressed and smiling; no need to look smart, but take the action to search for personal knowledge through risk taking.

Tangled expectations through the corner

The metaphor "dense fog" reflected my experience as a member, staff, researcher, scholar and learner, and contributor from Taiwan, who might be seen as insider, Taiwanese sibling, or outsider, family member or visitor. No matter what is perceived or identified, I would like to stay in the corner or move for new experiences. Also, I can be relieved to be used, or stand at the middle or freely leave the middle to find my determinations.

Summary and implications of the Group Relations conferences in China: Cross-cultural organisational development 2014–2021, Seth Harkins, EdD

It has been my privilege to organise and coordinate our Belgirate presentation on 31 October, 2021, and this chapter. We first began reporting our experience at the 2015 Belgirate Conference in our rendering of the 2014 Beijing GRC (Harkins et al., 2019). The above selfies by Jeffrey, Xioahua, Xumei, Nick and Kevin detail what has been learned from experience between 2014 and 2021. Their renderings reveal the crucial importantance of trust in the exporting/importing and transfer of knowledge of a Western model of group relations. This trust required considerable risking, vulnerability, trusting and resilience to learn about ourselves, each other, and our differences in language, culture and history. I have taken up roles as an SSG consultant, training consultant, researcher, associate director for research and mentor. Apart from my formal conference roles, I self-authorised as a researcher from 2014 to 2019. I took copious notes, conducted interviews, created, and administered Q Sort surveys, and took up a mentoring role with Xiaohua Lu in qualitative research and Xumei Wang in her quest for AKRI training and certification. The mentoring experiences have been marked by evolving and deepening trust central to our ability to explore our cultural differences and similarities, agree and disagree, and build a research colleagueship we expect to continue well into the future. As group relations practitioners we know this trust will oscillate but we have a foundation to always come back to as we continue to navigate the stages of trust.

As a group relations practitioner, educator and researcher, it has been important to me/us to document the evolution of group relations in China from 2014 to 2021. As Jeffrey Roth and Xiaohua Lu have related, the 2014 GRC enterprise began from scratch with literally no network, just the passion for group relations and a powerful belief that China would be receptive to this Western model. From a one-night stand, GRCs in China have grown into a committed relationship symbolised by the creation of an institutional holding – the China America Society for the Study of Groups and Organizations.

Over the past eight years we have amassed an enormous database regarding the development of group relations conferences in China including: field notes, conference brochures, fliers, emails, interviews, reports, Q Methodology studies and videos. Xiaohua Lu and I have partnered to publish two papers (Harkins & Lu, 2021; Lu & Harkins, 2021). With the privilege of leading a research team with Kevin Hsu in the online Wuhan GRC, we anticipate more publications in the future. Such work requires time for reflection and distilling of sensations, thoughts, feelings and projections. Several presentations of our longitudinal research have been made at the ISPSO Conference in New York in 2019, the AKRI Dialogues in 2019 and 2021, and now the Belgriate VII. From our research we have distilled eight stages of cross-cultural organisational development:

1. Germinating and networking
2. Infrastructure development
3. Training, launching, and organisational learning
4. Nurturing, ambivalence and splitting
5. Nurturing and rooting
6. Maturing and differentiating
7. Maturing, differentiating and anchoring
8. Autonomy and independence

As related above, GRC learning included pre-conference training and training conferences with two SSG training conferences, Beijing in 2017 and an LSG conference in Shanghai in 2019. Additionally, CASSGO has sponsored five online seminars since 2019. The organisational stages of development were significantly influenced by these training events, producing a talent cadre of Chinese GRC practitioners. Integral to each stage of development has been cross-cultural learning about trust and conflict. Learning regarding language and culture has also been crucial to this development, as conferences have matured from bilingual (Mandarin and English) to all-Mandarin conferences. As we look to the future, we anticipate the group relations ecosystem in China further evolving and contributing to global group relations development. We can expect the stages of trust to oscillate between calculation-based, knowledge-based and identification-based trust and further organisational differentiation and maturation.

References

Burke, W.W. (2018). *Organizational Change: Theory and Practice*. Thousand Oaks, CA: Sage.

Harkins, S. & Lu, X. (2021). Group relations in China 2014 to 2019. In D.E. Scharff (Ed.), *Psychoanalysis and Psychotherapy in China, 4*(1), 1–25.

Harkins, S., Huang, X., Jacob, S., Kennedy, D., Moore, V., Robertson, J., Roth, J. D., & Woon, J. (2014). Beijing group relations conference 2014: Cross-cultural learning and implications for the future. In E. Aram, C. Archer, R. Kelly, G. Strauss, & J. Triest (Eds), *Doing the Business of Group Relations Conferences: Exploring the Discourses* (pp. 145–169). London: Routledge.

Lewicki, R.J. & Bunker, B. (1995). Developing and maintaining work relationships. In R.M. Kramer & T.R. Tyler (Eds), *Trust in Organizations: Frontiers of Theory and Research* (pp. 114–139). Thousand Oaks, CA: Sage.

Lu, X. & Harkins, S. (2021). Trust issues in the development of group relations in China 2014 to 2018: Analysis and interpretation of key events, *Journal of Organizational and Social Dynamics, 21*(2), 250–282.

Ozdemir, H. (2015). Exploring group relations in China: Challenges, risks, and impact. In E. Aram, R. Baxter, and A. Nutkevitch (Eds.), *Group Relations Work: Exploring the Impact and Relevance Within and Beyond Its Network*. London: Karnac.

3

The Italian position/point of view

The true is the whole

Claudio Cassardo, Maria Pia Conte, Luca Mingarelli, Antonio Sama, Franca Fubini, Rossella Torretta, Louisa Diana Brunner, Chiara Ghetti, Elio Vera, Francesco Noseda, Pietro Catania, and Manuela Martelli

Introduction

Does a specific Italian identity exist within the GRC world movement? This question circulated among the 14 Italian participants at the Belgirate VII online Conference at the time of the Conference and also during the reflective work that the group carried on after the Conference. We have had regular online meetings.

The question is speaking to the relation between national identities and international groupings, between a fractal and the whole, between the local and the global. This is a theme that in the micro level is the tension and dilemmas between the singular and the plural, the individual and the group. The work that has to be done in order to adapt and include the individual identity in the group.

But it speaks also to the situated nature of the GRC movement and its relationship with the local and the global environment. The principles (the paradigm) and the structure (the model) of GRC have stood the test of time and space. The longevity, for example, of the Leicester Conference and the widespread presence of institutions and events linked to the GRC movement are testimony to the validity of principles and structure. However, each entity of this complex system has also "translated" the principles and model to the national culture and environment. It is this constant adaptation between global and local that has also contributed to the development and innovations within the movement. This chapter intends to contribute to the ongoing conversation both at international and national level.

The process of a group of eligible members of a Belgirate Conference, hosted by Il Nodo, who kept working through the experience of attending the Conference, has allowed the development of a process and a product. The product is the chapter that is here presented. The process is a group reflecting on the history, the development, the crucialities of the embedding of the GRC model within the Italian culture and environment. It has allowed Il Nodo to set up a reflective group that can support both the understanding of the impact of GRC on the national context and creating a shared knowledge that can contribute to the development of the institutions and its events while at the same time contributing to potential innovations.

Il Nodo Group manages GRCs and some applications for 24 years so far.

DOI: 10.4324/9781003502050-5

As a temporary conclusion, we can say that this process is mirroring, at national level, the process that Leslie Brisset has developed (after Belgirate 6) in the International Forum GRC. This chapter is a national contribution to that trajectory.

How the chapter is structured

This contribution derives from thoughts born in the group of Italians present at the Belgirate Meta-Conference, to reflect on our experience during the event.

We present the chapter as a talk that takes place at a table around which we are engaged in developing a reflection on Belgirate. Therefore, the chapter unfolds as if each of us were taking it in turn to speak in the first person.

This formula is a selfie about us because one of our themes is the question of the relationship between being individual subjects in a Conference and being a subsystem: speaking in the singular expressing a thought, whether shared or not, we think is a way of reflecting this theme.

Not only that, we believe this dynamic can describe an aspect of Italian-ness, namely our being at once a subject, a farmstead, a country and a nation, since time immemorial, and our inability to be primarily one thing or primarily the other.

We are not an "us" as other civilisations can be, and one of our themes is to reason about what kind of "us" we are. What kind of "us" I am.

Spirituality and the whole

A thought that a subgroup on spirituality at Belgirate helped me to have, is that when we speak of spirituality we speak of "an experience related to the insight of the whole", which is generated in moments of particular emotional availability, the sensation (which we sometimes call mysticism) of having a broader view, due not only to what you see from one vertex, but what you can see from several vertices at the same time.

A sensation comparable to the vase–profile experiment, imagining not seeing first the vase and then the profile, but seeing them together, a combined object, as Melanie Klein had decided to name the scene of the mother and father united in coitus as seen by a child.

Hegel had in mind that the man capable of seeing is the man who looks at the hour of sunset at the end of a day, the moment when you can see the day in its entirety just past; and that therefore to see it is necessary to fly at twilight, like the owl of Athena and like philosophy.

And again Hegel, at the head of his construction of a dialectic of history, said "the true is the whole": well, spirituality as it was treated at Belgirate in my feeling has to do with this theme, the theme of the whole.

And let us remember that this theme is indeed connected to one of the souls of the Conference, in the sense that a theoretical framework in which they are situated is the systemic framework, which constitutively has a relationship with the whole.

This aspect was immediately present in Belgirate when in the opening session there were comments about the "selfie" physiognomy of Belgirate, a word that for some sounded disturbing and for others sounded simple and clear, and for still others was heard in its entirety as both disturbing and simple and clear, with no need to take sides.

Choosing the word selfie, a way to describe the event at the same time disturbing and interesting, could be a good example of navigating towards ambivalence, and thus towards a spirituality of the event understood as the unconscious mandate to the participants to experience the simultaneity of points of view, even contradictory ones, the ability to see both from different perspectives in space and from different perspectives in time. That is, the ability to migrate simultaneously from one angle to another to see from different geometric angles, as in a dream, a waking sleep in the service of intuition.

In the wake of this, we have the chance to judge the Conference as an opportunity to grasp the beauty of ambivalence, and to pause in a place in which no one wins: a place in which the choice to consider the Belgirate event a selfie is not disturbing or fast, but is a new psychic object, combining these two emotional dimensions. Not merely simultaneous, but in unison.

The developments of the subgroup on spirituality, combined with the developments of the decision to call Belgirate a selfie, fostered in our group the idea of a connection between spirituality and ambivalence, or simultaneity of vertices. Not only that, but the relationship between spirituality and the whole, and between ambivalence and the whole, put in relation to the systemic framework that underpins a conference, leads to the hypothesis that its mission may be to help participants live in a humanism linked both to admitting our ferocity due to competition, and to adopting competition in order to cooperate. That is, to help participants experience the event in a state of permanent psychic duplicity.

I propose a type of pain and feeling formed when cooperation and competition come together, as can happen to two points of view that combine, an experience of paradox.

I used to think that the combination of vertices is the crucial ambition of those who organise a conference, for example the combination of the systemic and psychoanalytic vertices, within the more systemic task of using competition to foster cooperation, and within the more psychoanalytic task of helping people "see" the competition – struggling to prevent one vertex from winning out over the other.

We should note that to put at the same time the focus on spirituality or seeing the systemic issue of the whole from the perspective of spirituality is perhaps no coincidence that comes to mind for us Italians, immersed in a cultural and historical framework where the church has a crucial place, the pope has his home.

In this vein there is another thing I want to share: in Leslie's presentation the theme of fear of the other appeared, and in Dorothee's presentation appeared the Israeli man who, at a conference on the atrocities of Nazism in which a German colleague asks him, "what are you doing here?", replies "to meet your horror".

I suggest that this too is spirituality, and that spirituality is neither left nor right, but is in fact a whole, the outcome of a momentary insight, concerning the fleeting perception of the whole, like the sacred.

The question is how a conference can help its members to influence society, for example by bringing a reflection on spirituality not imbued with goodism, do-goodery, but endowed with an emotional neutrality that can be used to think about the world in a way that is not hampered by goodism.

In Belgirate 2018, I was part of a group of two on Spirituality. I can't remember what we thought then, now for me it has to do with acknowledging the coexistence of life and death, the mystery of how the matter I am made of can be alive and be me and will be dead and become no me.

We can call "integration" what we are calling ambivalence. Integration evokes an inner atmosphere of cooperation, while ambivalence evokes an inner atmosphere of competition. Our effort is to endure different perspectives.

In this vein, a further vertex for thinking the way towards wholeness is not so much to choose between these two conceptual scenarios but to look, both in the conference and in this group of ours, for the presence of two visions towards the inclusion–exclusion dynamic, where in one vision, differences, the "others" are a threat, and in the other are a value; but also the presence of a need, as Yossi Triest suggests, for these two visions to coexist.

The war of languages

Along the path of ambivalence (or of integration? Or of the inclusion–exclusion dynamic?), and recalling a comment made by Louisa Brunner during the event, on the fact that no one in Belgirate spoke of the fear and the aggressiveness present in the conference, I thought that perhaps no one speaks of it because it is convenient to show that I am not afraid, and that if it is not convenient it does not come to mind, as Darwin explained.

In this vein, a member looking like a hippie, with long white hair, very authoritative, suggested that in Belgirate the fear and violence present in the Conference were not being talked about even though they could be seen. He suggested that in the Conference they were talking about the war, but as an external phenomenon, whereas the mandate of a Conference is to see where the outside one is talking about is at the same time in it.

So then, from this perspective, the problem of a conference is to see where the massacre of the Jews that may happen to be talked about is happening here and now, and where, here and now, are the Jews and where are the "bastards"... where the things that are talked about during the event are also holograms of what is happening among those who are talking about it at that moment.

For example, a war to the death fought in Belgirate was the war of languages, the war of English, the overwhelming dictator, present all the time in two forms, spoken and chat. No one, apart from Louisa Brunner, was able to mention it, everyone too preoccupied with making a good impression to get out of "repression mode", a repression of the mandate and of the sense of the conference.

And, let's face it, the war was at the same time bringing (spiritually) in sight the other vertex, that one of the new pretenders, ungrateful, rude emerging groups.

This Belgirate was an interesting Babel without a God who knew how to give it a slap: no one who knew how to say to the English and the Americans "speak slower", or "... don't you understand that if you talk so fast I don't understand?" And who knew how to say to the non-English... "... but don't you understand that if you keep silent you agree with me? That you don't help me understand that I must go slower?"

In Belgirate there was the war of nations, mixed with the mission of getting work commissions and being chosen to do other future Conferences, and therefore with the mission of making a good impression on the most distinguished, mostly native speakers: and here is where the Conference is the society; here is where talking about corruption during the event was a way of talking about Belgirate and not just about bad guys in the society outside.

The Italian dilemma

In relation to this observation and in particular in relation to the issue of language, we Italians have to ask ourselves – and share this question with the system – how come we were not able to bring our voice more consistently and make this kind of comment during the event? How come a native speaker pointed out our silence?

This cautious attitude of ours has a historical connection with the Italian group's stance towards the Tavistock culture of GRCs, characterised for a long time by an attitude of a country subjected to a kind of colonisation, on the one hand wanted and desired and on the other hand feared and to some extent opposed, as explained in the chapter titled "Italian Group relation conferences between adaptation and innovation", by Brunner, Perini and Eva in the book *Adaptation and Innovation* (2019).

Not only that, but this edition of Belgirate, for the first time not held in Italy, is helping us to outline the Italian way of thinking about a Conference, either by renouncing to imitate the Tavistock parents, or by renouncing to run towards counter-dependency.

The character of the migrant

Another version of these observations on Belgirate 2021 can be seen in the character of the migrant.

Along with a high conceptual level of the content presented, I saw a difficulty to contemplate the diversity of the participants in terms of geographies, histories, cultures and lifestyles, and to treat them as opportunities to develop a broadening of perspectives and an experience of the whole.

This is a gap that Belgirate has produced in line with the splits that Europe is producing with respect to the migrant phenomenon. Being a migrant means leaving home and language to reach a new world, with suffering and violence connected to the change but necessary to adapt to the new culture and maintain one's own.

How did the system see this situation and how did it put it into play?

It was an event, this one, with many hosts and many foreigners (guests). But it was also an event where we were all migrants from our respective cultures and our common Conference experience to a new world of Zoom Conference.

It was an event with obvious elements of novelty, such as the variety of backgrounds and civilisations in the field, and such as the intrusiveness of the official language present, as mentioned, not only in one, but in two modes, verbally and by chat.

Belgirate, as a system, failed to intercept its feature as a traumatic event, neither on the part of the owners of the mother tongue, nor on the part of the babblers. The selfie did not show it.

To see the diversity and traumatic property of certain novelties, it is essential to recognise and suspend prejudice, to access the condition of precariousness and the sense of vulnerability. However, in the refugee camps, migrants are all placed together and the type of care they receive is the same, diversity is not contemplated.

So, Zoom, in the course of the event, was a refugee camp, a non-place, a place with no identity, a day after, without anyone taking care of it, i.e. without the system being able to access this data. On the contrary, the system has compactly contributed to the flattening and denial of this issue.

We Italians, for example, gradually found ourselves running alone, becoming solitary members of the event, and greeting our fellow migrants from the window, discovering ourselves to be a group and not just individuals only at a later date, in line with an Italian regionalist and rebellious tradition due to our aptitude for resisting the unitary paradigm, and building a "carbonara" culture against the invader, as our senior colleagues point out in their chapter, "Italian Group Relations Conferences between adaptation and innovation", in *Adaptation and Innovation* (2019).

During the event, we Italians had no group identity and many of us felt invisible. The way for the less experienced wing of us to be seen was to sneak into an empty space of words and try to say something in understandable English.

Native speakers were not attentive to this, a habit and deficiency no doubt driven by being native speakers. And we Etruscans were unaware of a belonging in which we were perceived by the system, which identified us as a country, not just as individuals. Unaware of how we lived and blind to how the system saw us, with the consequence that this impasse allowed the system not to question this aspect of itself, and to generate removal rather than learning from experience.

In this overall perspective, we Italians can reason about our identity and the existence of an Italian way of conceiving and organising a Conference by rethinking the character of the migrant.

Collusion instead of conflict

My non-anonymous entry into a Conference in the past took place in the free space, eating ravioli with a colleague saying "Come on Maria, there's more to Italy than just ravioli".

In Belgirate the atmosphere turned out to be different: our oscillation between being a colony and being an independent country here this year expressed itself punctually. Each of us was looking for a thought that would stand out in the conversation, with the fear of deviating from the prevailing conceptual atmosphere and at the same time with the anger of being excluded by the language, accentuated by the inattention of the native speakers, as if a projective cross-identification were at work whereby we Mediterraneans were again a colony invited to dine in the dining room of the masters, pushed into that scenario by their incomprehensible way of speaking, and they were again the masters pushed into that scenario by our way of falling into obsequious silence.

But a few things must be made clear. My gender, my sexual preference, the colour of my skin, my religious faith or non-faith, my genetic make-up, my nationality, my mother tongue, are my own personal issue. But if I use my traits to take advantage of other people through manipulation and bullying, that is a social issue.

Belgirate is an international event that chooses English as the lingua franca, and it is therefore up to the organisation to put people of different mother tongues in a position to understand each other. For example, the German colleague gave the presentation in English, accompanying the reading with the English writing clearly visible to all. Colleagues from England, Israel and the USA spoke off the cuff.

In this regard, I remember how I was struck by a person with mobility difficulties, who was interested in "Energy, creative collaboration and well-being in the organisations" – a Conference with a strong involvement of body and environment, conceived in Italy by Mingarelli and Fubini – when she pointed out to us that the flyer did not say whether or not there were architectural barriers in the place where the event would take place.

Let's learn again that a mission of the Conferences is to unveil differences as insights to be brought into the system, and at the same time to guard against the temptation to make them a reason for superiority.

The mind–body

I would like to express another thought on the Zoom version of the Conference, a "two-dimensional version" in the comment of many. Well, I have a different experience: I started using Skype 15 years ago when my first granddaughter was born, and while suffering its limitations, seeing each other on the screen over time has become a founding emotional scene of ours, an intense affective habit, a form of our love.

Emotions and affections have a physical counterpart in us in every way, whether we are in conversation with bodies in view or locked in digital cubicles. However, there was little talk of the body during the event, and I noted the strong difference between this event and the ECW event I mentioned, which was geared instead towards asking the body to be present in the scene of thinking.

So, moving from these observations we as the Italian subsystem can offer the Conference two suggestions.

First, a reflection on the system's attitude of safeguarding a power structure that corresponds to its founding act, and consequently a difficulty on the part of the system to construct a mixed culture both from the point of view of making all the languages in the field speak, and from the point of view of making all the civilisations in the field speak.

Second, a reflection on the extent to which the Conference is a device that resists the body and that prefers to preserve a Northern European, or at least Cartesian, attitude of mind–body dualism, rather than leaning towards a Spinozian monism, and a mind–body as one perhaps closer to oriental cultures and the south of the world, where it is warmer and one can live with fewer clothes on.

Without forgetting that we can consider mind–body monism, the endeavour to think of mind and body as a single act of living matter, resembles in some ways the endeavour related to seeking the whole, to seeking the spiritual and not only intellectual experience of seeing the same object from two sides at the same time, not first one and then the other, but both in unison.

And without forgetting that this impetus, being not only aimed at learning from experience, but aimed also at learning from ambivalence or multivalence (or from the Eros inherent in the "drive to integrate" fighting against the death instinct or against the "attack on the link") is a chance to study how to address in a Conference the problem of a language that is not only the mother tongue, but could be also the language of the brothers.

Some lines of reflection on the Italian perspective towards the Conference

We can begin to conclude by proposing that the Italian contribution to Conference culture lies in rethinking the myth of Babel.

Let us try to draw some further lines of reflection on the Conference from an Italian perspective that we discovered by working in this post-Belgirate group.

We reasoned that we as a group realised more fully that we were also a group, and not just individual participants, when someone in the Mat pointed out the silence of the Italians: this event retraces a complex history of the Italian journey in the Conferences, which developed from instances of admiration and imitation towards the Anglo-Saxon Tavistock culture, and has gradually moved, both with new initiatives and with multiple replicas of the GRCs in Italian as the first language, towards a progressive separateness, oscillating between a historical idealisation of the foreigner and a historical distrust of the foreigner, starting from Romanity up to the Marshall Plan.

One can derive an initial basis for reflection on Italian-ness by thinking that an experience present in Italian events and in our attitude towards Conferences is the discussion and experimentation on the horizontal nature of authority, more Mediterranean, as opposed to a vertical culture of authority, more Anglo-Saxon. The discussion on the extent to which our tendency to crack the verticality and lean towards the horizontality of the principle of authority is fostered by a history in which the Anglo-Saxon staff of consultants have presented themselves to us, Italians, also as the temple of an exclusive language, or is it due to our actual difference in the conception of entirety?

And we can derive another basis for reflection on Italian-ness by thinking that Italian events insist on a type of Conference less inscribed in a perfect, formal coherence, as happens in a spirit guardian of tradition.

In this perspective we can consider the opportunity that a selfie event like Belgirate could be organised in turn by each civilisation among those present, in the direction of developing an ambition towards the intuition of the whole.

Let us also reflect on the fact that our group could air these thoughts in Italian at a later date, and not in English during the Conference, protesting against the invader but behind his back, as we frequently have done for a couple of millennia.

It is worth asking ourselves how we can use this secular characteristic of ours to further the thinkability of the system and not just to further the enjoyment of the subsystem of our brothers, i.e. how we can use it to offer the system the Italian apex and not just to position ourselves in the system as a passive–aggressive little Italy.

And we can derive that a further basis for reflection on Italian-ness is to seek out how a Conference can make itself more suitable for reflecting the state of the world in which it takes place in real time, rethinking the theme of giving the structure more degrees of elasticity, both at the level of organising events, and at the level of rethinking the setting, bearing in mind that the concepts of authority and leadership in organisations are not abstract and ideal, but depend on the culture to which they belong.

And one last suggestion, in line with the themes of the I–us, the insight of the whole, sensory spirituality, learning from ambivalence, migration, unison, and the body–mind: an Italian approach to the Conference, a contribution to the Conference that can come from a theoretical perspective that is very much alive in Italy, in the Italian psychoanalytic community, which is to encourage the sharing of the reveries that are gradually present in the minds of the participants, as Bion spoke of them first and then his later interpreters, Ogden (1997a,b), Grotstein (2000), Ferro (2008), Foresti (2008) and Civitarese (2016), as an element that, together with Social Dreaming, can help the system to stay asleep in order to dream and not just stay awake in order to think.

But, finally, a point we have to share with the system on the Italian position concerns the working group that created this chapter, and the similarity between this group and the text. We are a group of people very different in the degree of experience towards Conferences, in the type of training (psychoanalytic for some, systemic or sociological or economic or articulate for others), in ages, visions, conceptual and political preferences. Moreover, a salient characteristic of this group and a reason for its differences is the presence in it of several generations, which may be equivalent to several dialects (which, let us remember, in our country have always been real languages until a handful of years ago), in full line with the tradition of our culture, which is a culture of the communes, not a culture of the state. It is a culture of districts, of contrade (city districts), of campanili (bell towers). Italy as a whole is younger than California.

In this furrow, for some of us the theme of the struggle of languages and the theme of the colony are not salient, and have not been felt at all, while for others of us they have; and for some of us the use of ambivalence to think about the relationship with the whole has been adequate, while for others of us it has not, in relation to our different backgrounds. And yet we have decided to guard this text precisely because of the decision to expose ourselves with a text that is imperfect, but suitable to represent us as a working group and as a subsystem engaged in studying its own difference and the way to transform it into a cooperative turbulence to be offered to the system.

Conclusions

The group we formed allowed us to reflect on our identity, on the Italian position towards the Conferences. We used the following themes: spirituality, migration, mind–body unity, the war of languages, the colonial atmosphere, the horizontal physiognomy of the principle of authority, the here and now as a priority.

In particular, we developed these conceptual lines: spirituality understood as the experience of the simultaneity of points of view; migrancy understood as an experience and metaphor to indicate the state of mind salient in a Conference and salient in our current humanism; mind–body unity understood as an experience constantly present in a Conference, but obscured in favour of intellectualism; the war of tongues understood as a version in the Conference of the struggle for power that animates human life; the colonial atmosphere understood as the Conference's attitude to which the founders and colonies contribute through an unconscious collusion; the horizontal physiognomy of the principle of authority understood as the need to study the participants' relationship with the staff, not only with the classical scheme of verticality; the here and now understood as the Conference's essential mandate to search for the link between what is discussed and what is experienced during the event, which is often, however, abandoned.

The experience of working to find our own Italian position also helped us to see how this position is sustained by a paradox whereby drives to be united in order to recognise ourselves under the same identity "tent", help us to feel our own territorial reach within the Conference and coexist with drives to be different among ourselves, to have different views, more belonging to different regions than a single country, and helped us to reflect on how we place ourselves on the axis of inclusion–exclusion, on how much we are willing to include differences, and consequently on how much we know how to compete in order to cooperate, and how much, on the other hand, we are inclined to fight them and compete to win.

References

Brunner, L.D., Perini, M. & Vera, E. (2019). Italian group relations conferences between adaptation and innovation. In E. Aram, R. Baxter & A. Nutkevitch (Eds), *Adaptation and Innovation: Theory, Design and Role-taking in Group Relations Conferences and their Applications* (pp. 73–88). London: Routledge.

Civitarese, G. (2016). Reverie and the aesthetics of psychoanalysis. In D. Blue & C. Harrang (Eds), *From Reverie to Interpretation: Transforming Thought Into the Action of Psychoanalysis* (pp. 39–53). London: Karnac.

Ogden, T.H. (1997a). *Reverie and Interpretation: Sensing Something Human.* London: Karnac.

Ogden, T.H. (1997b). Reverie and metaphor: Some thoughts on how I work as a psychoanalyst. *International Journal of Psychoanalysis*, *78*(4), 719–732.

Ferro, A. (2008). Trauma, reverie, and the field. *Psychoanalytic Quarterly*, *77*(3), 905–993.

Foresti, G. (2008). La costruzione del 'terzo orecchio'. Ascolto psicoanalitico e setting interno dell'analista in una prospettiva storica. *Gruppi*, *3*, 11–26.

Grotstein, J.S. (2000). *Who is the Dreamer Who Dreams the Dream? A Study of Psychic Presences.* Hillsdale, NJ: The Analytic Press.

Part II

Locating Directorship and Leadership

Introduction to Part II

This part explores aspects of leadership and how it is experienced in the directorship of Group Relations Conferences and in relation to experiences of Belgirate VII. The chapters in this part share observations on Group Relations in how identity and context can inhibit the ability to take up leadership.

In the chapter "Too Black to lead: When authority trumps race?" Mary Fullerton and Urban Hudlin explore the relationship between race and leadership and how it is taken up in a Group Relations conference. Can localised generational trauma impact the way a conference develops and can be led? Delving into the layers of race and identity as it shows up in a colonialised context. How do the echoes of history impact not just what can be said but also what can be tolerated and who is given – even tenuously – access to power? The journey Fullerton and Hudlin take us on creates the space to consider how reflections on the "there and then" often collide with conversations taking place in the "here and now". This chapter fuses these experiences together and forms new meaning.

In "The Director's experience of postponing a conference", Louisa Brunner explores the parallels between the isolation of the COVID-19 experience and the invitation to take up a director role at international conference. She reflects on the question of where our boundaries exist, whether they are internal and external, physical or imagined. The challenge of melding aspirations with the shadow of perceived failure allows us to consider what it is like when we achieve our goals, or have to face when we don't. Alongside these reflections, Brunner considers the emergence of a new space online for the practice of group relations is central to this exploration.

"Sibling relations as an extension to group relations selfie" is a chapter in which Smadar Ashuach and Simi Talmi explore both the significance and relevance of sibling relations to the dynamics of relationship in a range of contexts, asking the question whether the importance of siblings has been overlooked by Freud due to his own difficulties with siblings. They introduce the concept of the "Law of the Mother" exploring the impact of female authority and ideas of protection that are associated with it. How does the idea of female authority, when combined with the responsibilities of containment impact wider society and the restricted space of Group Relations conferences?

DOI: 10.4324/9781003502050-7

The final chapter in this part, "Spotlighting corruption through the Group Relations lens – a selfie", the authors explore the impact of known corruption in Israeli society. They consider the question not if there is corruption, but, rather, how it can be understood and explored, and what it represents for our society. Can flaws and failings in leadership be accepted or should they be rejected by the collective? The challenge of balancing humanity and the inhuman expectations that come with leadership is a complex discussion. This challenging chapter also considers to what extent the use of our GR methodology and tools can aid us to gain a better understanding of corruption. It also explores what enables the avoidance or ignoring of the impact of the phenomenon of corruption not just in society, but within the field of Group Relations.

4

Too black to lead

When authority trumps race?

Mary Fullerton and Urban Hudlin

Since 2018, Caribbean Group Relations Consulting has worked in partnership with the Tavistock Institute of Human Relations to deliver group relations conferences for the Caribbean. The first conference took place in the context of the significant political upheaval when the leadership of the Trinidad and Tobago government was under scrutiny for corruption and various other ethical challenges.

It emerged that in 2014, there was an issue about race within the Trinidad and Tobago leadership, and the phrase "too black to lead" was levelled at a political candidate, which was deemed too hot to handle in the group relations conference. During an election campaign in 2014, Fitzgerald Hinds, a former senator of Dr Keith Rowley's political party, the People's National Movement (PNM), was reported to have said that persons within the ranks of the political party claimed that Dr Rowley was "too black to lead". The report also claimed that former PNM ministers and business people aligned to the PNM agreed that Dr Rowley was too dark in complexion to become prime minister. It is not clear whether the statement was used to win the votes of people of African origin or that Hinds was confronting "racial" tensions within the PNM party.[1]

Again, in the 2019 group relations conference, the issues of race were alive and challenging to leaders across the public and private sectors. The Conference Director, who was black and from the UK, wanted to use the term "too black to lead" and explore what it might mean for the conference in its context. However, it was felt by the Trinidadian local staff that this was not appropriate, and the nuances of race and the culture dynamics were too complex to be addressed in a three-day group relations conference.

As 2020 arrived with the full impact of Black Lives Matter in the USA, emerging also in Trinidad and Tobago, it was clear that the race dynamics in relation to police brutality, while not directly transferable to Trinidad, highlighted that the same processes of brutality and marginalisation were apparent. The police officers, indeed the whole policing system, was led and staffed by black people.

This chapter seeks to explore, with the Belgirate participants, the Trinidad and Tobago Group Relations experience of the nature of the authority invested in roles and systems, and what is unspeakable in our view of history and patterns of behaviour. We will further consider race relations and the tension between the racialised

DOI: 10.4324/9781003502050-8

bodies of those in authority positions and their relatedness to their primary task. Is it possible that black and brown police officers have similar degrees of hatred toward their black and brown citizens as white police officers do? What can a group relations lens open up and bring into focus for policy and practice in matters of policing and race, or systems of legal processes and race? The 2020 Conference had to move online and even then, as the first non-USA black-led conference, we would have a chance to see if it was viable, or would the embedded racism in both black and white people unconsciously frustrate recruitment? The Trinidad conference did occur on 28–31 October, 2020 as planned. Was it possible that the issue of race wanted to announce itself in the system?

Trinidad and Tobago, twin islands in the southern Caribbean situated off the north-eastern coast of Venezuela in South America, is approximately 1,981 square miles, with a population of 1.4 million persons, according to a United Nations estimate in 2020. This twin island has its beginning as a plantation economy, a slave and indentureship society, nurtured in colonialism. It is a diverse, multiracial, multiethnic society with mixed races. Europeans, Chinese, Syrians, Lebanese and other mixed races make up approximately 20% of the population, while the two major races, Africans and East Indians, each being approximately 40%.[2] The first prime Minister, Dr Eric Williams, in his Foreword to *History of The People of Trinidad and Tobago*, was convinced that the division of the races was the policy of colonialism and integration of the races was the only way for transformation of the society (Williams, 1963). This is embodied in the national anthem's line "here every creed and race find an equal place". David Rudder, in 1999, envisioned the two major races living in harmony using a connection of the two main rivers in Africa and India, in his calypso 'Ganges and the Nile'.

Rudder paints an idealistic picture of race relations in Trinidad and Tobago; however, this is not our lived experience. This songwriter accurately captures our superficial self-presentation, which tends to be couched in humour and lightheartedness. In fact, this is a thick mask constructed as a mechanism for survival. The annual Trinidad and Tobago carnival, calypso (which is commentary in song) and some of our Caribbean literature, clearly all speak to the daily masquerade as our way of being for survival. The leadership of Trinidad and Tobago and the leading institutions are governed by persons of colour. However, the system unconsciously continues to maintain a colonial mindset, a culture of subservience, with the control and power of a minority.

Struggle, slavery, indentureship

The Africans brought against their will and the subsequent systematic human degradation suffered, as well as the multiple ethnic groups which arrived, feeds into the notion that indeed the Caribbean was never meant to be a dynamic human society. It is simply a location in which the economic ends of the colonisers were satisfied by whatever means possible. The great suffering is the conceptualisation of self-hood in a society which has come into being through an accident of history.

Caribbean historian Kortright Davis claims that imprint of plantation life, with its system of domination and absolute control, exploitation and violence is engrained, so that even today the society remains a plantation (Davis, 1990, p. 35).

The abolition of slavery act in 1833 saw the arrivals of indentured labourers. In the minds of the British West Indian planters, who at this time had tried several immigration schemes in order to find the most suitable labour force, believed that the East Indians were cheap and controllable. Approximately 147,900 Indians were brought to Trinidad from 1845–1917 and were assigned to work in the rural areas on sugar, cocoa and coconut plantations.[3] The Africans left the plantations, settled in the urban communities and were employed in the public service and police service.

Imitation

For a long time, the Caribbean context has been characterised by a belief that importations of ideas, mode of dress, values, goods and customs are more valuable than whatever is present locally. To some degree, Davis attributes this psychological disposition to the basic internal operations of the colonial system of 'divide and rule'. He believes that the rigid social stratification and weak community structure is a consequence of the plantation mentality, which was carefully instituted by colonial masters. This strategy inculcated a sense of natural inferiority which systematically alienated people from their 'cultural endowments' (Davis, 1990, p. 35).

The issue of imitation goes beyond mentality. According to Professor Bridgette Brereton (2011), the school system established immediately after emancipation modelled and imitated the English schools. The school curricula were essentially British and this has basically remained the same until very recently. In all areas of life, from culture to sport to governance, Trinidad and Tobago followed whatever was done in the Empire.[4] The gestures of imitation are glaring and they continue to play an influential role in present day life.

Coloniality

The history of colonisation is such that the imagination of people has been dominated by systematic repression, which in turn has robbed them of modes of knowledge, symbols and the instinctive embrace of their own images and beliefs in the transcendent. For social theorist Quijano, colonisation succeeded in the creation of a system that deprived peoples of legitimacy and recognition, thus leaving colonised peoples in a state that continued to be dominated by European cultural patterns. Colonisation ends but coloniality continues (Quijano, 2010).

Coloniality refers to the conceptual ideology which began in the New World and extended globally. It is the basic principle within the exploitation of people which fuelled the colonial machinery. It denotes a political and economic relationship in which the sovereignty of a nation or people rest on the power of another nation. This model of power emerges as a result of colonialism and determines culture, labour and knowledge. Coloniality, therefore, is not merely the residue of colonial relationship but is connected to the establishment of forms of domination and subordination which were very important in the socio-historic setting of the New World. This "ideological matrix", according to Quijano, has been extended globally and provides the underpinning for what we know today as modernity (Quijano, 2010, pp. 22–24)

Colourism

Colourism is a new word in the Caribbean lexicon. The term, coined by Alice Walker, has gained notoriety in the social sciences and Caribbean Studies in the past 45 years.[5] The experience of colourism has had a much longer history in Trinidad. Colonialism was the main vehicle for perpetuating this phenomenon and our history traces colourism as a by-product. The repeated sexual abuse of women slaves resulted in the birth of children with a lighter skin tone. These children experienced a less horrid existence as they enjoyed the privilege and protection of the master. The historic roots of this socio-cultural reality continue to function within the social dynamic, the result of which is a more subtle form of discrimination. The colour of a person's skin legitimises authority. This is an underpinning of the colonial machinery that influences life and leadership today.[6]

While these are the facts, colourism is referred to as a form of prejudice in people who may belong to the same ethnic group but within that group are treated differently because of their skin. Sadly, the darker the skin tone the more likely is the person not to be accepted into particular social circles. The lighter skin tone has greater access and acceptability. Colourism in Trinidad and Tobago is experienced within and by all races and has implications for housing, business, media and political leadership.

Race as a political tool

In 1956, the first Prime Minister, Dr Eric Williams, identified himself as African, formed a political party, the PNM, with mainly African members, with his focus on the challenges of coming out of slavery. The Indian community felt their interest were excluded from the interest of the PNM and so formed their own political party. The distrust between the Africans and Indians was already complex by history, location, language and job opportunities. This was fuelled by Dr Williams at a public meeting in 1958 when he blamed the Indians for the PNM's loss of the federal elections. He believed the Indo-Trinidadian community to be an angry and recalcitrant minority which presented a danger to the progress of the country. They are an impediment to the West Indian advancement (Ferreira, 2017, p. 163). The use of race as a political tool to win votes continues today by both major political parties.

What does this Trinidad Group Relations experience tell us about the nature of the authority invested in roles and systems and what is unspeakable?

Group Relations in Trinidad and Tobago is in its infancy. During the preliminary preparation for the first conference hosted by Caribbean Group Relations in 2018, we were given the basic information that almost 20 years prior, group relations conferences were led by two white male Europeans, who partially followed the Tavistock methodology. They held at least five conferences in different Caribbean territories. Moreover, two of the present staff members of the 2018 conference were part of the staff of that early iteration. Caribbean Group Relations, in its focus to present the group relations experience, and to witness its impact in the Caribbean, accepted the basic disclosure of these prior conferences, as information offered.

During the first staff meeting of the 2018 conference, a metaphor of a stolen baby was used by those staff members of previous conferences to express dissatisfaction and distrust with the "ownership" and authority of group relations in the Caribbean. '... you, Indian woman, took away our baby, the baby of us black women ...' Our subsequent staff meetings and two later conferences were intense and combative, due in part to the perception that the new leaders of group relations did not have the authority to lead.

What does this experience of group relations tell us...?

"You have taken our baby...". What do we know about the babies of slaves on the plantation? It has much to do with ownership. The baby, although gestated in a black womb, belongs to the master. For a birth mother to claim ownership is out of order, and for a father to name that baby is totally unacceptable. Neither mother nor father have the authority. The baby belongs to the plantation. Caribbean Group Relations was opening up without realising it, a painful memory, an unconscious flow of beliefs and assumptions about leadership. First, the historical acceptance and legitimacy of white authority and second, suspicion of black leadership.

Interestingly, the group relations conferences 20 years ago were led by two white males in authority, now being represented as the standard, by two black women. The black women were accusing the new leadership of taking their baby. Is it possible that the two members were being used by the conference in the here and now organisational system to mirror a deep unconscious wound? Is the pain of losing a baby to be interpreted as an articulation of the unconscious unresolved trauma that the system had consciously refused to explore?

The staff members have been in the company and tutelage of white leadership who had symbolically handed on the baton to these two members after the Europeans left. Did the staff members unconsciously see themselves as the experts unwilling to authorise the new local organisation or black leadership to represent group relations in the Caribbean? In the LSG of the conference, it had been observed that participants unconsciously looked for direction from the white British consultant, and did not recognise the black British Director in role. One staff member confirmed that in this society there is an unbridled acceptance of white leadership and suspicion of black leadership. To the white consultant, who was anxious on entering the small group study system for the first time, it was said by a staff member, "You don't have to worry about what you say or do, just show up, they will love you."

This unconscious position of authority and ownership of group relations conferences in the Caribbean was so pronounced that the two staff members convened meetings to begin a new group to manage group relations in the Caribbean two months after the first conference, in 2018. Another attempt was made three weeks after the second conference in 2019.

How do we explore the tension between the racialised bodies of those in authority positions and their relatedness to their primary task?

We shall adopt two approaches, Quijano's articulation of coloniality and Bion's (1961) basic assumptions. This will aid our understanding of authority and the emotional dynamics, including unconscious patterns of behaviour in the system.

The theory of dependency as introduced by Quijano offers as a key concept "coloniality of power" (Quijano, 2010, p. 25). It speaks of race, labour, space and people according to the needs of capital to benefit the ruling class. Coloniality of power produces distorted paradigms of knowledge, the result of which brings about colonial difference and further creates "coloniality of being" (Escobar, 2010, p. 39). Colonisation succeeded in leaving colonised peoples in a state that continued to be dominated by European cultural patterns and the supremacy of whiteness. The cultural patterns most citizens within a post-colonial environment adopt continue to be aligned with those of the colonial office or mindset.

The first prime Minister of Trinidad and Tobago, Dr Eric Williams, 1962–1981, expressed coloniality in this way. He said there is always competition for gaining approval of the colonial office or those in authority. "In this climate, political rather than physical, social climbing has become the major industry of Trinidad and Tobago – invitations to cocktail parties, and appearing in photographs and social columns of the newspapers". He went on to say, "some of those who protest against colonial exploitation seek in the same breath to demand the perquisites enjoyed by the expatriates. Political, Trade Unions and professions are riddled with individualism" (Williams, 1963, p. 281). Imitation is founded on the premise that the act in itself renders the actor authentic. This is an illusion; in fact, the act speaks to a profound lack in the actor which only accommodates superficiality. Eric Williams hints at the inauthenticity of leadership based on the imitation model. For Williams, this model seeks "identification" with success in the primary task.

Is it possible that black and brown police officers have similar degrees of hatred toward their black and brown citizens as white police officers do?

Based on our history and ethnic composition there is no surprise that there are no white police officers in our law enforcement. While the levels of brutality visible in the USA are mainly white officers exercising power over black people, in Trinidad and Tobago black police officers exercise similar use of force on persons who look like them. This issue is systemic. Slavery and indentureship caused intergenerational mental anguish. It was a system which subjugated.

Considering the trauma experienced by people as a result of our colonial history, what possible impact might this have on subsequent generations? Melanie Klein's object relations approach can aid our understanding. Klein says the infant can experience fear and joy in relation to the same object. For Klein, the infant takes in data from the external environment and develops a mechanism for its own survival. Here the infant does not experience its body as a whole but fragmented. This is mobilised by anxiety regarding loss of internal objects. The police officer is not exempt from the trauma of colonial brutality. It is internalised. The trauma of colonial history is unresolved. In our present day the excessive use of force and brutality are still being exercised by police officers. The authority vested in them by the state legitimises their actions.

With reference to police violence to persons in depressed areas, could the brutality and hatred be emerging from the police officers projecting what they could have become, and the fear of the consequences for persons who they are connected with in some way and who look like them? The infant in Klein's view sees objects, not persons, and relates to that object. The object to which the infant relates is the mother's breast. Mother is therefore split into the 'good breast' or the 'bad breast'. The good part is idealised and the bad is persecutory. In this sense the infant employs a process of introjection and projection to keep good and bad parts separate. The infant projects its love, hate and feelings of ambivalence into the breast. Moreover, anxiety is intensified, thus the object is experienced as persecutory.[7]

In Trinidad and Tobago, the manifestation of such violence is not new. In 1937, 25 years before our Independence from the British, Corporal Charlie King, a black police officer authorised by the Colonial Office, was set on fire when he was sent to arrest Butler (a black representative of anti-colonialism) at a public meeting. Corporal King, fearless in his approach, was acting on the power and authority of the Colonial Office, was treated with the hatred that the black gathering had for the colonial office. Here, a self-authorised black leader authorised a black group to prevent a black police officer from carrying out the responsibilities of white authority. Based on this experience, is it possible that authority trumps race?

What can a group relations lens open up and bring into focus for policy and practice in matters of policing and race, or systems of legal processes and race?

Trinidad and Tobago is a multifaceted society where the citizens were historically divided by race for political power and economic gains by those in authority. Group relations will show up the conscious and unconscious dynamics within the system. It will help citizens experience themselves in role in the multiple complex relationships that they encounter in their daily lives, their anxiety triggers, how they influence others, how they are influenced and some of the obstacles to decision making and execution. The group relations methodology will be useful in the exploration of how behaviours, decisions and outcomes are influenced in society.

We know from Freud (1900a) that there is no time in the unconscious. This helps us to understand that what we are experiencing now, namely, our inability to speak out, is firmly entrenched in our psyche. The earlier statement made by Senator Hinds was responded to in this way by Sir Ronald Sanders, Jamaican Observer:

> Of all the offensive — and unintelligent — statements made in the politics of the post-independence Caribbean, an assertion that Dr Keith Rowley, the leader of the opposition in Trinidad and Tobago, is 'too black' to be prime minister, has to rate as the worst. It is a telling indictment of the person through whose mind the thought passed without perishing and from whose mouth the stupidity was uttered.

This statement shows that race as a sociological construct and the tension involved has been a difficult horse to mount, as also experienced in our exploration of using race as a theme for the Caribbean conference.

With regard to policy, it is worth noting that during the early post-colonial period Trinidad and Tobago witnessed the discarding of voices that opposed the views and policies of the first Prime Minister, Dr Eric Williams. According to Ferdie Ferreira, an adviser to the then Prime Minister, any criticism or objective analysis of problems, both in the party and in the country, is considered an attack on the Prime Minister, his Cabinet colleagues and the Government. Clearly the resistance to speaking about race or opposing views to those in authority, such as the legal system or policing, is very much embedded in the system.

Plantation life was marked by subservience. Several theorists, including Freud, Klein's object relations and Bion's basic assumptions, help us to explore the culture of dependency, pairing by having to take a side or divide and rule, and fight/flight in our suppression of speech, humour and masquerade. These behaviours are crucial strategies for citizens' survival, which have given way to mistrust, unhealthy competition and corruption, as we say locally, "climbing on each other like crabs in a barrel".[8]

The 2020 Caribbean Group Relations Conference, "Authority & Role: Disruptive Caribbean Leadership", experienced the disruption in technology at the beginning of the conference. This triggered anxiety and anger in the membership, resulting in indictment of the system as being upside down, with the insecurity that the system would not be able to hold the group because of incompetency of the leadership. The leadership is disappointing and screwed up. Plantation leadership and the trauma being experienced is not of the past but is present in the conference with the fear of a black male and an Indian woman as leaders in the system.

The group flight to safety was by looking for the arrival of birds, wanting to be lively, singing a happy song or to be on a beach. The group engaged in phantasies about Caribbean rules of interaction and culture such as 'anytime is Trinidad time", including associations with drinking and dancing. This was an online conference with participants from different places and different races. Membership space was prime for group survival. You are either in or out. There was grave anxiety about not being able to get into the space; at the same time there was the sense of being alone among many, with no privacy and loss of identity.

The pain of history and the risk of speaking the unspoken was loud. Members experienced grief from what the group felt would not be said, and the loss for what would not happen. Because of diversity there was the need to "bite the tongue" and be considerate at the same time as 'Will what I say be heard, but not as I want it to be heard?"

The group experienced skin colour as getting in the way, with the association to privilege and perceptions. Is racism only about black and white persons? Some parts of the group felt 'erased' and relegated to observer status, while at the same time holding the fantasy that they were expected to take sides.

Racism is not simply about the individual in isolation, but what they experience in a social context. The language of race is used to manipulate persons and resources in order to maintain power and control. The attempted conversations involving race were choked by anger and frustration. The system did not allow speech to occur. This raised a few questions, such as: what part of oneself must be given up to nurture the system? What privileges does the white person have to give up; how are those who are Jewish but considered white related to by a black person?

Too black to lead when authority trumps race?

In Trinidad and Tobago, speaking out on race and authority has political and economic consequences. The expression by a public official, "too black to lead" escaped for a moment from a deep unconscious space only to be repressed by the media, local and foreign, including the BBC, and the general public who rejected the statement.

Corporal Charlie King, a black policeman, authorised by the colonial office in his effort to arrest Butler, helped us to understand that authority takes precedence over skin colour. Corporal King relied on the authority given by white leadership and was fearless in his action to arrest Butler. The people, in their hatred for the colonial office, authorised themselves to take violent action against a black person, King, the representative of the colonial office. Authority trumps race.

We acknowledge that this exploration was limited in many ways and gives only a snapshot of much wider systemic issues. Economics, imitation and coloniality are embedded in the system. Caribbean history testifies to economic power holding the authority. Trinidad and Tobago is a unique society that is multicultural and multiethnic, diverse by race, geography, alignment and many more grey lines. The country has been led by black leadership since its independence, and continues to be divided, with many black persons suffering injustice. In this country, is it that authority trumps race or is leadership and authority influenced by race?

References

Brereton, B. (2011). Spain in Trinidad: A presence and absence. *Express* newspaper, 13 October, accessed 15 October, 2021.

Bion, W.R. (1961). *Experiences in Groups*. London: Tavistock.

Davis, K. (1990). *Emancipation Still Comin'*. New York: Orbis Books.

Escobar, A. (2010). Worlds and knowledges otherwise: The Latin American modernity/coloniality research program. In D.W. Mignolo & A. Escobar (Eds), *Globalization and the Decolonial Option* (pp. 33–64). New York: Routledge.

Ferreira, F. (2017). *Political Encounters, 1946–2016.* Ferdie Ferreira.
Freud, S. (1900a). *The Interpretation of Dreams. S.E., I.* London: Hogarth Press.
Quijano, A. (2010). Coloniality and modernity/rationality. In W.D. Mignolo & A. Escobar (Eds), *Gobalization and the Decolonial Option* (pp. 22–32). New York: Routledge.
Trinidad and Tobago Population 2022 (demographics, maps, graphs). Available at https://worldpopulationreview.com (accessed 15th June, 2022).
Williams, E. (1963). *History of the People of Trinidad and Tobago.* London: André Deutsch.

5

The director's experience of postponing a conference

Louisa Diana Brunner

Introduction

I live in Milan, Italy, the first area in the Western world to be hit by COVID-19. There is a before and an after in our lives. Before it was unthinkable, impossible to mentalise, that a pandemic could happen in the vibrant, dynamic Milan; the virus was far away, it belonged to the "others". It was in China, it was in distant East Asia.

At the end of March 2020, on a Sunday afternoon, I was sitting at home in a completely empty Milan where all was silent and still. Only the sirens of the ambulances taking people to the nearby hospital could be heard. I felt that death was penetrating through the glass panes of my windows. It was very unsettling and frightening. Probably many of you have had this type of experience at the time or sometime later when the COVID-19 pandemic hit other countries and the world.

In that period, I got the Youtube video, https:www.youtube.com/watch?v=1u85mY0J3NQ. The video is a series of images of an empty Milan during those times, with the music of "The Sound of Silence" (Simon and Garfunkel, 1964), which has become my leitmotif, or symbol, of my experience at the time, my scene. The places shown in the video are my places, they are extremely familiar in my daily life, they are around the corner of where I live. I felt "lost in familiar places", as the title of Shapiro and Carr's (1991) book states. An *unheimlich* experience. I played it hundreds of times, I shared it with many family members, friends and colleagues. I cried many times looking at it, thinking of the loss we were going through. I felt silenced, I lost my voice, my creativity. "We were astonished and unable to understand what had happened, we could not see how vulnerable we were, and still are" (Capua, translation from the television programme *Di Martedì La7*, 26.10.2021).

In this context of the lockdown, in August 2020 I was supposed to direct the PCCA (Partners in Confronting Collective Atrocities)[1] conference, "Walls, Open, Closed, Sliding: Europe and Our World Today in the Netherlands". Fakhry Davids was the Associate Director. Living in a virus front-runner country, quite soon I became aware that we could not hold the conference. We could not take the responsibility for members and staff. I had several conversations with the PCCA management committee and with the Board until it was decided to postpone the

DOI: 10.4324/9781003502050-9

conference. We did not cancel it. I was immediately also asked as Director to think about some recommendations for the next conference, and this gave the idea of the continuity.

What did it mean to postpone the 2020 PCCA Conference, sponsored by an organisation called Partners in Confronting Collective Atrocities involved in working with societal traumas and conflicts? The atrocity of the virus was among us. Were we victims of an invisible perpetrator (an unusual *Other*) that we never thought we would have to confront? What happens when trauma becomes viral?

This chapter is an opportunity to reflect, to think through and share a very powerful personal and professional experience. Therefore, it is not an academic chapter, but more of a self-portrait vignette or an autobiographic/ethnographic narrative within the systems-psychodynamic/group relations tradition.

So, first I briefly present my conceptual framework: trauma, mourning and loneliness, after which my experience on taking up the role of Director and of the postponement is discussed, followed by how the conference developed in 2021, and finally my experience of the presentation itself at the Belgirate Conference 2021.

Trauma, mourning and scenic understanding

The literature on trauma, loss and mourning is immense and impossible to summarise. I will just put forward some conceptual ideas from some authors who have accompanied me on this reflective journey. Furthermore, I will present Lorenzer's concept of *scenic understanding*.

Trauma

During the first months of the March–June 2020 lockdown, I attended many online events about what was going on. I needed to make sense of such an unexpected situation and to connect to friends and colleagues because I felt isolated, locked in my flat or quarantined (Brissett, 2021). I felt nurtured by the possibility of staying in contact with my community, with my world, although limited by the online dimension, a new territory for all of us, which I really liked. Is it relationships or a relatedness in the digital space? In terms of sense-making, the only way of describing what I was and what we were experiencing, emerged during an OFEK meeting when Avi Nutkevitch defined it as a trauma. Why hadn't I thought about it? This is evidence of how we defend ourselves and how trauma impinges our capacity to think, symbolise and mentalise and it is an attack on our attachment system (Lemma & Levy, 2004).

In Greek, τραῦμα means wound, damage and it is a central psychoanalytical concept.

Erlich (2020, p. 1) argues that trauma is an "elusive" concept difficult to capture and very much discussed. Differently from other psychoanalytical ideas trauma includes both the external and the internal realities, for example the mind-body relationship. Trauma is "inflicted and renders the unfortunate object as its victim" (Erlich, 2020, p. 3). He (2020, p. 9) continues, "trauma is thought to operate by breaking through normal adaptive and defensive capacities and paralyzing the ego functioning". It has to do with the death instinct and "not being". Trauma depends on individual resources.

Mitchell (2003, p. 9) suggests that trauma leaves "a gap within". Gould (2004, p. 14) states it also impinges the capacity of "... making of appropriate links, both internally, to the traumatising event itself, and often to others. For example, survivors most commonly do not share their experiences, even with those closest to them". A traumatic event remains related to the past, not connectable to the present, a sort of untouchable "ghost" (Coles, 2011) in the wardrobe which needs to be kept separate.

Mourning

Interestingly Freud developed the concept of mourning, in *Mourning and Melancholia* (1917e) during the First World War, when people were dealing with a lot of losses. He addressed the impact of external events on the psyche that leave "the individual severely, possibly permanently impaired" (Lemma & Levy, 2004, p. 7) and can lead to mourning or to melancholia. Since spring 2020 we were going through the most significant global crisis since the Second World War. It was a time of loss of many loved ones and all other kinds of losses on a massive scale. My feeling is that all this has not been worked through and mourned, and if it cannot be worked through then the consequences will deeply impact the next generations.

Jacobi (2005, p. 1080) says,

> The work of mourning is a set of mental processes conscious and unconscious, initiated by the loss of an emotionally and instinctually cathected object. Once this work is complete, the subject is gradually able, within a period of time that cannot be shortened, to separate from the lost object.

Mourning for example leads "to the loss of interest in the outside world, the loss of capacity to love, and the inhibition of all the activity". Furthermore, there is "a withdrawal of the object libido and the dismantling of all the bonds that have hitherto united subject and object ..." (Jacobi, 2005, p. 1081).

Hall and Stokes (2021) argue that loss is

> When life disrupts our accustomed sources of purpose and meaning, we need time to find new sources if we are not to sit in a fog of denial. Holding on to the familiar, a kinder way of describing resistance to change, is what the brain is designed to do even if the mind is willing to move forwards... changing this is disruptive and uncomfortable.

Winnicott (1954) suggests that mourning has to do with those processes which have a favourable outcome that leads to "relinquishing the loved object". Bowlby, 1960, p. 10). does not agree and suggests that mourning is "a set of psychological processes set in train by the loss of the loved object irrespective of their outcome".

Bowlby (1960, p. 14) also describes grief as "the subjective experiences that follow loss and accompany mourning".

Scenic understanding

Lorenzer is a German post-Frankfurt School cultural analyst and psychoanalyst, not much known outside Germany since his work was not translated from German until recently. He used a hermeneutic process of psychoanalysis to analyse "cultural phenomena" (Salling Olesen & Weber, 2012, p. 19) in empirical qualitative research. He developed the idea of *scenic understanding*, which I have found helpful in this work.

Lorenzer argues that the unconscious is not only an individual dimension, but also a social one in terms of "socially produced, non-verbalised meaning, a complementary dimension of culture and symbolic expressions – including language use – that are products of both conscious and unconscious processes" (Hollway & Jefferson, 2013, p. 29). A scene can be seen as an intermediate area and "an affective and embodied register of meaning" (Bereswill et al., 2010, p. 225), an area between "subjective fantasy" and "concrete social reality" and it is in this space that he located *scenic understanding* (Hollway & Froggett, 2012, pp. 3–4).[2] Lorenzer invites us to pay attention to the significance of the "provocations" in the scene and to our emotional and affective responses to them. These "provocations" have not only an individual meaning but can also have a collective meaning since "the subjective fantasies draw on the necessarily social quality of collective experience embedded in interaction forms" (Hollway and Froggett, 2012, p.5.)

I have used *scenic understanding* in my PhD research and on the basis of my practitioner consultancy experience, I think *scenic understanding* can be very helpful also in my practice and I have adopted it to understand what I went through in postponing the conference.

In this chapter's introduction, I described my scene at the beginning of the lockdown in March 2020 and spoke about the video that I watched so many times featuring an empty Milan within the music of "The Sound of Silence" (Simon & Garfunkel, 1964). That was my scene, my scene that I tried to understand through Lorenzer's lenses, not only individually (my own experience) but also socially (the broader collective meaning of that experience). As mentioned above It was a time of loss, grief, mourning of many loved ones, often without the ability to pay one's last respects, and all other kinds of losses. Our old familiar world and much that we used to take for granted are now in the past, and anxiety, disorientation and uncertainty still confront us in the present. Different people reacted differently to the lockdown. Some were very active and creative (I felt very envious of that energy), others, like me, were paralysed and felt silenced (the sound of silence). I could not write or be creative, I could only try to survive what we were going through. Certainly, work with clients helped me and also taking care of daily life. For example, my energy was lower, especially in any writing activity. I felt wounded. At present I still feel the consequences of the lockdowns and these very difficult years. In a way I was "contaminated" by the virus. Also writing the presentation for the conference and this chapter hasn't been easy. It is so difficult to go back to those terrible months in 2020 and only the deadline of the conference and of the book have obliged me to sit and write, but with a lot of effort and pain.

Taking up a director's role

Taking up the director's role has a lot of implications. I will briefly describe the itinerary as it customarily occurs in Group Relations, and I will illustrate what has been my itinerary for the 2020 PCCA conference and the online 2021 conference.

I made a limited literature review about this specific role. Little has been written about the director's job description and competences. This impressed me, considering the importance of this role in the conferences. Here are just some examples of papers among the few I was able to find. A.K Rice (1965) sets the stage and gives some important inputs. Josselson et al. (2015) discuss the experience of co-directorship. Aram (2012) shares her fast-track experience in "Climbing fast up the ladder" to directing the Leicester conference. Interestingly, in recent times, more has been written on the administrator's role than on the director's one.

A conference director is authorised by a sponsoring or organising body through a complex selection process that involves competences, skills, institutional politics, country, affiliations, relationships, etc. It is an important step in terms of delegation of authority, responsibility, accountability and trust. The type and level of authority and decision making which is delegated to a director and what pertains to the sponsors is an issue not openly discussed but essentially ruled by custom and practice. This can easily create some ambiguities and conflicts between the director and the sponsor about authority boundaries. On the basis of my personal experience, I think that a conflict between the director and the sponsor can be healthy and generative, but it needs to be worked through and addressed. Finally, it also has to do with the ownership of the conference; who is the owner, the director or the sponsor? Furthermore, the director's authorisation depends on her/his internal authority ("from within", Obholzer and Roberts, 2019) and of the staff and participants ("from below", Obholzer and Roberts, 2019).

Trying to make a summary of the complex role of a conference director, my understanding is that the director:

- Has the overall responsibility and accountability of the conference, staff, members, venue
- Is in charge of the design of the conference
- Chooses the staff
- Takes care of marketing tools – flyer, brochure, website, design
- Provides the structure (design and technology) and content food for thought and working hypothesis (containment)

It is necessary to add that the financial liability of the conference is that of the sponsor/organising organisation, while the director monitors the budget. Some directors or some administrators are involved in preparing the budget and are accountable for it. I do not agree with this approach, because I think that the sponsors' involvement in terms of responsibility in this matter is fundamental.

The search for the location/venue, marketing and recruitment can be a joint and a collaborative venture of the sponsor/organising organisation and the director, and also the sponsors should participate in this responsibility.

The director's role requires, on the one hand, leadership, entrepreneurial, managerial, marketing, political and, nowadays, technological capabilities and competences. On the other hand, it requires systems-psychoanalytical and Group Relations conferences experience and competences such as boundaries and time, management, containment, negative capability, reflective stance, emotional intelligence, interpretative stance, etc.

I will now try to portray my selfie of how I took up my role as Director in 2020 and 2021. At the time I had already directed three Group Relations conferences in Italy in 2005, 2008 and 2009 and a PCCA conference in 2018 in the Netherlands. In the Italian experience I always had a challenging relationship with the sponsors, experiencing their relating to the director as a "delegate" and not a "plenipotentiary" in my taking up of the role (GRC language).

The 2020 PCCA conference and the postponement

In 2016, I was quite smoothly authorised to direct the 2018 European PCCA conference, "Exclusion, Resentment and the Return of the Repressed: Europe in a Globalized World". I considered it a great honour and the accomplishment of my desire to direct an international conference; I was very energised and excited. I was the first non-psychoanalyst after Eric Miller to direct the conference. The authorisation for the 2020 conference was a bit ambivalent in my opinion. In 2016 we had not made an agreement regarding how many conferences I would direct, so I did not know if I would direct the 2020 conference. Instead, the PCCA board took it for granted that I would direct again. Furthermore, the PCCA tradition had always been to run a conference every two years, but in 2019 we had had a different conference of the so-called Nazareth series, "80 Years Later, Will History Repeat Itself? The Fallout of the Holocaust on Those Affected, Looking Back, Moving Forward", directed by Mira Erlich-Ginor. This meant holding a conference every year. I was in full agreement about it, but some change was going on in the system.

Once authorised, I decided to innovate the 2020 conference by forming a training group with associate consultants to support the development of a new generation of PCCA consultants. I worked on recruiting the staff, on the website and the brochure, on the design and on the budget in collaboration with the PCCA treasurer. The title was "Walls – Open, Closed, Sliding? Europe and Our World Today" and it was planned again in the Netherlands at the end of August. Everything was ready in January 2020: as conference management we had started to meet regularly each week. Recruitment felt slightly slow, and although it was too early to really assess it, I started to get very anxious about this. Two of my main sources of anxiety in directing a Group Relations conference. The first one is recruitment. My feeling is that, in our community, if you do not recruit, it is perceived as a failure and it is a means for the evaluation of the director. It could be my personal representation, but I am not sure. During the conference itself, my main concern is containment and casualties, also due to lack of containment.

My engagement, investment and commitment, together with the Associate Director and the Administrator was high. Nevertheless, I felt a dark cloud hovering over the recruitment. Had I been too innovative by having Associate Consultants? Was the conference too expensive? Was it a repetition of the 2018 conference or too near to the 2019 one? All this was in my mind at the beginning of 2020. I had the feeling something was not going so well. Furthermore, I felt my energy lower than in the previous times, I did not know why. I have always believed that a conference depends very much on the energy of the director and I was worried.

As a colleague suggested, the decision and the process of postponing or cancelling a conference depends very much on the director's identity, personality, culture and country. In my case it was strongly influenced by the fact that I was living in the first western and European country affected by COVID-19, as described in the introduction to this chapter.

I had several conversations with the PCCA Management Committee and the Board. At the end of April 2020, it was decided to postpone the conference. It was a very painful decision both for PCCA and for me, also because the conference was due in August which was still quite far away. The responsibility towards members and staff and the deadline for confirming the hotel influenced our decision. But we did not cancel the conference. I was immediately also asked as Director to think about some recommendations for the next conference in 2021 and this gave the idea of the continuity. At the same time, I invited the Associate Director to continue our work together.

Postponing or cancelling a conference is very difficult for any director: it raises all sorts of feelings, it is against the nature of the job. So, I thought that describing the experience of postponing the conference due to an event such as the global pandemic, which was affecting everybody and was beyond our responsibility (we did not market the conference badly, we didn't recruit, etc.), would make the task easier to open a discussion about issues that seemed unspoken.

Once the decision to postpone the conference was taken, I was able to take care of the practicalities quite easily, but I could not think about the future. I had to mourn the *baby* who never saw light, the *baby* whom I had carried in my mind for a long time. I was in a bereaved state of mind. Thinking it over, probably we decided to postpone the conference, symbolically, to avoid an *abortion*, which would have been more painful, and to build on the work that already had been done.

What did it mean to postpone a conference sponsored by an organisation called Partners in Confronting Collective Atrocities? The atrocity of the pandemic was around us, we were victims of an invisible perpetrator (an unusual and unexpected "other") and the trauma was viral. I could not really find what was specific to postponing a PCCA conference compared to an ordinary Group Relations one. I suppose that the pain of the director and the complexity is the same as in Group Relations conferences. A hypothesis can be found in the title of the 2021 conference described in the next section.

The 2021 online PCCA conference

In summer 2020 we considered holding the conference again in the Netherlands or in Germany, but in the autumn of 2020 COVID-19 hit us again and we were locked down. I felt that we needed to have a European conference again in 2021 and the only territory I was able to think of at that stage was the online one. We dared to pursue this venture. The first PCCA online conference took place from the 8th to the 11th April, 2021.

Our conference was a postponed conference but, interestingly, differently from the European Football competition, the Olympics and many other events in 2021, we called it the PCCA 2021 online conference and not the 2020 conference taking place in 2021 and online. Although in 2020 our lives had to change dramatically and we had to adjust in order to, survive physically and mentally, we believe that there is a "before" the pandemic that still exists, there is a "present" that we have to manage as best we can, and there is a very uncertain future.

The overall vision and strategy of this conference was: tradition and innovation, back to the origins and a launch into the future, trusting the method. Much emphasis was given, on the one hand, to the founding elements of the Nazareth–PCCA project: *Working Through the Aftermath of the Holocaust, The Past in the Present, The Repetition of the Past* and *the Work in the Presence of the Other* (your enemy or somebody with whom you are in conflict). Another aspect that was addressed was that the conference is a fractal of the society in which we live. Therefore, the experience and the dynamics that develop within the conference space should also re-enact what is taking place at an individual level, in groups, organisations, institutions and communities – we are part of a broader societal level outside. This process aimed to help us understand and learn what is happening here and out there in Europe and in our world today, both *above the surface* (immediately visible) and *beneath the surface* (the covert and unconscious dynamics) and to support us in our role of citizens in our daily life.

A conference, even an online one, can be seen as a transitional space in Winnicottian terms, where members can experiment creatively with new learning, also by taking up different roles. In order to be able to offer a safe enough space and in consideration of the intensity and depth of a PCCA conference, our main concern was containment for staff and members. But how to do it online? The real challenge was to provide the necessary containment and holding both through the structure (the design and technology) and the content (in terms of food for thought and working hypotheses).

The title was "Walls – open, closed, sliding? The virus, Europe and our world today". The same title as in 2020 but with the addition of the word "virus", which in itself is an atrocity. Perhaps we were able to use the word "virus" so blatantly in the title thanks to PCCA's longstanding experience in dealing with trauma and collective trauma. The virus, and the pandemic, is a different atrocity from the Holocaust or a terrorist attack or others – it is a global trauma. We could not work *in the presence of the other* our enemy, because it was an invisible other and we were online. Nevertheless, our PCCA experience was helpful and applicable in this new context. It will take many years and generations to understand how its aftermath will be and how we all have been affected.

From a systems-psychodynamic perspective, a hypothesis can be drawn. In 2020, we introduced a training group of Associate Consultants. The 2021 conference took place online and, due to the complexity of the new technological dimension, we did not plan to have Associate Consultants; it was too much innovation at the same time. This mirrors how much students availing themselves of remote learning at all levels suffered and lost during the pandemic. The new generations are the most affected by the pandemic in terms of their future life. The fact that the virus did not allow the 2020 conference to take place can be seen as not giving this space for learning to the new generation and to the future.

The Primary Task of the conference was: To provide a space for participants to explore how issues around the theme "Walls – open, closed, sliding and the virus" play themselves out in the conference itself, and in Europe and in our world today in general.

We had the same staff, except those who could not make it, the same layout for the flyer, the same website with a different text, with an emphasis on the 2020 conference. Although extremely new in terms of space and place, it was not a new conference, it was a resurrection of the never born 2020 one.

Differently from the 2020 conference, recruitment was smooth. Interestingly, in the first days when we opened registration, many people registered, so we were very soon aware that the conference could take place. But then recruitment stopped so we decided to extend the early bird fee for a further two weeks. From that moment the flow of registration became continuous until the day the conference started. We had 65 members from 21 countries. The online dimension allowed us also to accommodate last minute registrants. Since we were recruiting very well, another staff member was invited to join the conference a few weeks before the conference started, and he kindly accepted with very short notice.

Some themes emerged in the conference

- Although online and mediated by technology, a deep sense of connectedness developed in the staff and in the membership
- The theme of the virus COVID 19 emerged largely in the smaller groups and in the Social Dreaming Matrix

- From members' feedback there was surely a lot of personalised learning
- Overall in the conference it was more difficult for members and staff to work on the systemic and societal dimension, except in the SDM where, as a staff member noted, the collective was presented through metaphors. This could also be due to the strong psychoanalytical tradition with its founding element on the individual and large psychoanalytic membership of PCCA conferences that permeates the PCCA culture
- The issue of identity and the complexity of identity boundaries associated with the multilayered nature of identity (personal, political, national, racial, geographical, sexual, gender, etc.)
- Minorities, especially from Eastern Europe, found it difficult to find a "voice" that could be heard. The members who were represented more in numerical terms, such as Germans, had a louder voice. This also mirrors East–West power dynamics in Europe.

Finally, the *baby* was able to come to life at last and it was a nice one. A pioneering culture and atmosphere due to a post-traumatic survival state of mind and the new online dimension deeply shaped this conference. It felt like a regeneration experience. There was a lot of energy, commitment and engagement in the work. It made me think of myself as the first born in a family of Holocaust survivors and the atmosphere I breathed in my childhood.

Another scene accompanied me at that stage: a "Perfect Symphony" by Ed Sheeran and Andrea Bocelli (https://www.youtube.com/watch?v=eiDiKwbGfIY&ab_channel=EdSheeran). It made me think about *re-generations. Re-generations* is a word that does not exist, but it wants to integrate the idea of a regeneration and the relationship among generations like the "Perfect Symphony". *Re-generations* is about the future, about collaboration and the shared lived experience among generations, diversities, cultures, races, languages, etc. The 2021 online PCCA conference experience gave me hope in the future, especially in the new generations. PCCA conferences and GRC conferences can play an important role, by offering important platforms, places and spaces where one can explore unspeakable and difficult topics. They can also support a better understanding of the world, in which we live, being more equipped and aware of the conscious and unconscious dynamics at stake.

The experience of the presentation in Belgirate 2021

To conclude this chapter, I share some thoughts about my experience of presenting at the Belgirate conference. My expectation was that a certain number of conference directors would attend, and I was looking forward to engaging with them in a conversation about taking up this role (was it my ambition or excessive expectation?). Instead, I had a rather limited audience; there were some conference directors, but not many. It was a lovely, welcoming, very appreciative audience, I was really grateful for, and satisfied with, the experience. Nevertheless, I asked myself what was going on systemically in the Belgirate conference, and I wondered why the presentation did not attract a larger audience.

I have some hypotheses. First of all, it confirmed that talking about the experience of taking up the role of the director seems difficult in our community. As mentioned above, there is evidence in the lack of literature on this aspect of the Group Relations conferences since their inception. In Latin there is a saying, *Nemo Profeta in patria* (nobody is a prophet in his country). Group Relations conferences were developed to study leadership, authority and organisation, but it seems difficult to engage with this in our own "country", in our leadership roles.

Some feedback I got from the colleagues attending the presentation was that it was so moving. This made me think that by describing in words, images and music what had happened in 2020 when COVID-19 and the lockdown started, was very/too painful – memories of what we had been confronted with re-emerged by going back to that traumatic period. My overall experience of the 2021 Belgirate conference was that there was a hyperactive, manic defensive atmosphere avoiding acknowledgement of why we were online and going back to those terrible times, which my presentation was reawakening. It was better to stay far from it. All Belgirate conferences are a competitive environment, but the 2021 one was especially so and I hypothesised that it was another way to avoid the pain of our condition at present and the traumawe had gone through and which we are going through.

Furthermore, after the conference, all the Italian colleagues who attended the conference met. For the first time we were a large contingent. This made me think about my Italian nationality. Chapter 3 in this book is by my colleagues (with also my more external participation), who discuss the experience of being Italians in detail. The impression we shared, albeit considering the differences among us, was that we were pushed into brackets. We had lost the venue in Belgirate, the place and space after which the conference had been named. We lost our voice; our language was not understood. New languages were heard more; also, our language, our identity, our Italian-ness felt as if it were in the background of the actual interest. Was my presentation and was I part of this dynamic?

I am grateful for having been able to attend the 2021 Belgirate conference, to present at the conference and to write this chapter, to have had the opportunity to reflect on an incredible experience and to have been nurtured with so much food for thought.'

Notes

1 https://p-cca.org/ As it states on the website "PCCA works towards developing strategies to engage with the legacy of past atrocities that can contribute to opening up the possibility of a more hopeful future. The aim of the organization is to work through the effects of the Holocaust and of past and present national and international conflicts that lead to destructive escalation, in the service of a better understanding among national groups worldwide". The core activity is the PCCA conference.

2 As Hollway and Froggett (2012, pp. 3–4) argue, "There is some convergence between Lorenzer and Winnicott ..., on the significance of the intermediate area of experience. For Winnicott (1985[1971]) this is a "third area between that which is subjectively conceived and that which has the quality of externality".

References

Aram, E. (2012). "Climbing fast up the ladder?!" The lived experience of directing. In E. Aram, R. Baxter & A. Nutkevitch (Eds), *Group Relations Conferences Tradition, Creativity, and Succession in the Global Group Relations Network.* Abingdon, UK: Routledge.

Bereswill, M., Morgenroth, C. & Redman, P. (2010). Special Issue: Alfred Lorenzer and the depth-hermeneutic method. *Psychoanalysis, Culture and Society, 15*(3), 221–250.

Bowlby, J. (1960). Grief and mourning in infancy and early childhood. *Psychoanalytic Study of the Child, 15*: 9–52.

Brissett, L. (2021). Beyond an eye for an eye: Identity, relatedness and digitisation during the pandemic. Presentation at OFEK.

Coles, P. (2011). *The Uninvited Guest from the Unremembered Past.* London: Karnac Books.

Erlich, S. (2020). Whose trauma Is It? A fresh look at an elusive concept. Unpublished paper.

Freud, S. (1917e). Mourning and melancholia. *Standard Edition 14*, pp. 243–25.?

Gould, L.J. (2004). Collective working through: The role and function of memorialization. Paper presented at The Austen Riggs Center, Erikson Institute Fall Conference, "Lost in Transmission: An Interdisciplinary Study of Trauma Across Generations", 16–17 October, 2004.

Hall, J. & Stokes, J. (2021) *Changing Gear: Creating the Life You Want After a Full-on Career*. Headline.

Hollway, W. & Froggett, L. (2012) Researching in-between subjective experience and reality. *Historical Social Research/Historische Sozialforschung*, pp. 1–14.

Hollway, W. & Jefferson, T. (2013). *Doing Qualitative Research Differently: A Psychosocial Approach* (2nd edition). London: Sage.

Jacobi, B. (2005). Mourning. *International Dictionary of Psychoanalysis*, 1080–1082.

Josselson, R., Khaleelee, O. Sher, M., Mc, Rae, M. Chattopadhyay, G., van Reeckum, G. & Long, S. (2015). The experience of co-directorship in group relations conferences. In E. Aram, R. Baxter & A. Nutkevitch (Eds), *Exploring the Impact and Relevance Within and Beyond its Network* (pp. 181–2006). Routledge.

Lemma, A. & Levy, S. (2004). The impact of trauma on the psyche: internal and external processes. In S. Levy & A. Lemma (Eds), *The Perversion of Loss: Psychoanalytic Perspectives on Trauma* (pp. 1–20). Whurr.

Mitchell, J. (2003). *Siblings*. Cambridge, UK: Polity Press.

Obholzer, A. and Zager Roberts V. (Eds) (2019). *The Unconscious at Work. A Tavistock Approach to Making Sense of Organizational Life*. London: Routledge.

Rice, A.K. (1965). *Learning for Leadership Interpersonal and Intergroup Relations*. London: Tavistock.

Salling Olesen, H., & Weber, K. (2012). Socialization, language, and scenic understanding. Alfred Lorenzer's contribution to a psychosocietal methodology. *Forum Qualitative.*

Shapiro, E.R. and Carr, A.W. (1991). *Lost in Familiar Places: Creating New Connections Between the Individual and Society*. New Haven, CT: Yale University Press.

Simon, P. & Garfunkel, A. (1964). "The Sound of Silence", written by Paul Simon, and released by Columbia Records, New York City.

Winnicott, D. W. (1985[1971]). *Playing and Reality*. London: Routledge.

Winnicott, D.W. (1954) The mind and its relation to the psycho-soma. *British Journal of Medical Psychology, 27*(4), 175–272.

Sibling relations as an extension to Group Relations selfie*

Smadar Ashuach and Simi Talmi

Introduction

My four-year-old grandson, whose brother is four years older than him, sulkily walked up to his father and said: "I'm very angry at you!!"

The father, in wonderment, asked, "Why?"

The son replied: "Because you married mum and now I don't have anyone left to marry!" and began crying bitterly. Left with no other options, the boy responded to himself: "Fine, I won't be a dad, I'll be just a brother."

One of the lacunae in psychoanalytic thinking, which is a key theoretical source of the systemic-psychoanalytic/psychodynamic approach, lies in the almost complete absence of reference to sibling relations and their impact on one's inner world and psychic development. Even when sibling relations are addressed, they are usually discussed merely as a displacement of parent–child relations. This fact is particularly intriguing, since we tend to spend more time, as children, with our brothers and sisters than with our parents. Moreover, our relationship with our siblings lasts longer.

Conceptualisation and exploration in classical psychoanalysis revolve around the vertical parent–child relational axis and the Oedipal myth as an organising principle. Meanwhile, the horizontal sibling relational axis is left virtually unattended.

Where have the siblings gone in psychoanalysis?

This question gains even more importance when we consider that the Bible's first murder is a fratricide (Cain killing Abel) rather than a patricide. Furthermore, the entire book of Genesis is laden with stories about complicated sibling relations: Jacob and Esau, Joseph and his brothers, Isaac and Ishmael – and the ripples of these relationships live on in the collective memory of most peoples to this very day.

* This chapter is based on Ashuach, S. and Talmi, S. (2022). "The Law of the Mother and its expression in group relations conferences and organizations" in S. Ashuach & A. Berman (Eds), *Sibling Relations and the Horizontal Axis in Theory and Practice* (p. 171). Abingdon, UK: Routlege.

DOI: 10.4324/9781003502050-10

This lacuna is, most probably, no coincidence. We present several conjectures that potentially explain the absence of references to sibling relations in psychoanalysis, drawing on the works of Prophecy Coles (2003) and Juliet Mitchell (2003) as well as the importance of linking the two axes – the vertical parent–child axis and the horizontal sibling axis – on both the actual and phantasmatic levels, as relational axes that affect psychic development from birth. We would also suggest that these two axes of influence and the matrix of their encounter are relevant to the understanding of group relations conferences and society.

Freud and his brothers (as analogous to Joseph and his brothers)

We often witness an interesting connection between a thinker's biography and the key notions of the theory they put forth. History tells us that Freud had a complicated and uneasy relationship with all his siblings. Freud's mother was his father's third wife and 20 years younger than him. His father had two other sons from his first marriage and Freud's relationships with his half-brothers were very volatile and filled with hostility and hatred. Consider the famous story about the nanny at the Freud household, who was very close to Freud – as a child, he loved her dearly and was very attached to her. His half-brother saw the nanny stealing something from the house and immediately ran to tell his parents – probably as a result of his strained relations with Freud – and the parents kicked her out of the house. Freud took her dismissal and their separation very badly and never forgave his brother for it.

History also tells us that Freud was the apple of his mother's eye. She loved and adored him and he grew up as "mother's little baby": she would call him "my golden Sigi" and shower him with love. Eventually, she became pregnant and gave birth to Freud's baby brother, Julius. Freud had a hard time accepting the arrival of this new baby and developed a hostile attitude towards him, as the one who deprived him of his status as "his majesty the baby".

His younger brother Julius died of an illness when he was eight months old. Freud felt guilt over his death and was certain that his hatred had killed his baby brother. In the famous letter he sent his friend Fleiss, in which he wrote about discovering the Oedipal complex, Freud also shared the death wishes, hatred and envy he had felt towards his little brother, Julius, as well as the guilt he had to endure for feeling, after baby Julius's death, that he had "finally gotten rid of the little intruder".

Freud also had complicated relationships with his sisters.

Those who argue that Freud does not completely ignore the subject of siblings in his writings are indeed correct. In his canonical 1921c publication, *Group Psychology and the Analysis of the Ego*, Freud describes the relations and identifications of the sons with their father, who is the leader, and the affinity between the sons–brothers. He nevertheless resolves the competitiveness, hostility and envy between the sons–brothers, which bear a homicidal potential because each of them wishes to exclusively possess the leader, through a reaction-formation mechanism: hostility is turned into a relation of powerful fraternal identification. Freud does not elaborate on the dynamic of sibling relations in and of itself, focusing instead on their relation to the great father–leader.

This tendency to overlook the influence of siblings on one's world and psyche is also manifest in the case studies written by Freud and his followers. In many of his case studies, Freud makes a point of mentioning that the patient has siblings, but leaves this information as mere background and refrains from exploring its emotional significance and its effects on the patient's inner world. For example, in the case of Little Hans, Freud mentions that a little sister was born and the fact that Hans is now angry because he is given less attention – but this line of thought is not developed any further. The entire case is analysed and discussed solely in light of the Oedipal conflict. Once again, we see Freud's caution and avoidance when facing the emotional upheavals involved in the birth of a new sibling and the complex relationships between siblings.

If we believe in the impact of the unconscious on our lives, we must enquire about the absence of siblings in psychoanalysis.

To what extent has this intricate saga of sibling relations in Freud's life influenced the psychoanalytic doctrine he developed and the central importance of the vertical and triadic axis (father–mother–child) alongside the almost complete disregard for the effects of the horizontal axis (sibling relations) on emotional life? Could this disregard be unconsciously related to Freud's family history, as presented above, and the way in which Freud internalised his experiences with his siblings as self and object representations in his inner world.

But, perhaps the reason for Freud's almost complete disregard of sibling relationships in psychoanalysis involves the universal fantasy of exclusivity, the narcissistic desire to be the only child. Support for this hypothesis comes from Freud's discussion (1916–1917) of three blows that humanity has suffered throughout its development:

> The first was when they [humans] learnt that our earth was not the centre of the universe but only a tiny fragment of a cosmic system of scarcely imaginable vastness. This is associated in our minds with the name of Copernicus, though something similar had already been asserted by Alexandrian science. The second blow fell when biological research destroyed man's supposedly privileged place in creation and proved his descent from the animal kingdom and his ineradicable animal nature. This revaluation has been accomplished in our own days by Darwin, Wallace, and their predecessors, though not without the most violent contemporary opposition. But human megalomania will have suffered its third and most wounding blow from the psychological research of the present time which seeks to prove to the ego that it is not even master in its own house, but must content itself with scanty information of what is going on unconsciously in its mind.
>
> (Freud, 1916–1917)

We suggest that the awareness of the existence of siblings – of others who are like me – is analogous to the Copernican revolution: a grave narcissistic injury to the phantasy of being the one and only, singular and exclusive. It is, in fact, an unconscious phantasy – "phylogenetic inheritance" (Klein, 1952), as Melanie Klein claims, or a preconception (Bion, 1961) of the desire to be the only one, and the special one, in the whole universe (and not just in the Oedipal triangle) and the human narcissistic injury to discover that there are others like me and I am actually part of a series like me. Psychoanalysis may have unconsciously colluded with this universal narcissistic wish and the injury that its relinquishment entails, resulting in the marginalisation of siblings in psychoanalytic discourse.

It is our contention that this narcissistic wish, while it may vary in intensity, perhaps precedes the Oedipal fantasy developmentally.

The past two decades have demonstrated a growing interest in sibling relationships, in their significance and unique impact on psychological development, beginning early in life, as either actual or imaginary primary objects.

Juliet Mitchell (2003, 2006, 2018), one of the leading analysts exploring this field, views the birth of a sibling (both actual and phantasmatic) as an emotional psychic event that bears the marks of an actual, independent and emotionally constitutive trauma.

The trauma, sibling trauma, is an emotional experience that is charged with feelings of hatred, envy, competition, and murderous rage alongside attraction, desire, sexuality, love, and greed.

When my younger son was nine years old, he asked to speak to my husband and me. He sat us down and then explained how and why we would never understand his position. He is the youngest of four while my husband and I are the eldest in our family. Everything he does has been done three times before him. And every one of his inventions his siblings are able to improve on. So, what is his uniqueness?

In Mitchell's view, the psyche develops through vertical and horizontal relationships that intersect and are interchanged in unconscious psychological life, much like the dynamic relationships between Klein's positions (the schizoid–paranoid and depressive positions) (1952). The vertical axis involves generational differences, hierarchic distinctions, totemic, and the taboo on patricide and incest; that is, the law of the father. The horizontal axis is based on our relationships with others who are in a position similar to our own (such as siblings, colleagues, and peers). Time and again, this axis brings us face to face with the loss of our status as the exalted baby and the trauma of the transition from being "the baby" to being "a baby". The horizontal axis involves the necessary acceptance of oneself as an ordinary person. This acceptance does not mean that the individual is not unique; rather, it means that all brothers and sisters are both ordinary and unique. The transformation of the self is gradual and endless. Its failure is manifested as distress, disturbance, or madness in an antisocial child. Such an emotionally charged relationship leads Mitchell (2018) to propose the law of the mother as a function that seeks to regulate, contain, and organise the emotional intensity in sibling relationships and protect children from the potential of real or symbolic fratricide or incest.

What does "the law of the mother" mean?

In addition to the mother's containing and holding function on the vertical axis, she plays a key role in organising the horizontal axis between siblings, which she does in two central ways. First, by recognising each of her children as a unique individual with distinct contributions and singular differences as well as by acknowledging those parts which the children share and have in common. The mother loves her children because they are hers, but recognises their respective uniqueness.

Second, by imposing prohibitions in the home against violence and incest between siblings. The mother regulates intersibling hatred, allowing them to overcome their envy and rivalry in a safe environment. Thus, she facilitates the infant's growth into the social order.

In fact, the law of the mother is a parental function that does not necessarily reference the mother's gender identity.

We suggest that the theory of sibling trauma and the law of the mother as described by Mitchell (2006, 2018) can enrich our understanding of the processes that take place in group relations conferences, in organisations, and in society at large, and by this enrich our Selfie.

In group relations workshops there is a special emphasis on the relations to the authority. We suggest that at the same time the encounter with others (participating siblings) also holds a field of complex relations that are reflected in the emerging dynamics; understanding it enriches our Selfie.

Examples of the collapse of The Law of the Mother in Group Relations conferences

An international Group Relations conference

In February 2020, at the beginning of the COVID-19 global pandemic, the last (to our knowledge) international group relations conference was held. The OFEK Group Relations Conference began when the world's first restrictions were instituted to help mitigate the spread of the virus. A week before the conference, people arriving from China were banned from entering Israel, so two attendees from China had to cancel their participation. Calls came in from Israeli participants seeking to confirm that no attendees could spread the disease. The conference team decided to operate according to the guidelines released by the Israeli Ministry of Health. Thus, on the opening morning of the conference, a participant from Singapore, who was not subject to quarantine, was permitted to attend, but the participant's presence raised the anxiety level both within the conference team and among the other attendees.

The question that dominated the conference from the beginning was whether the group was protected adequately from the coronavirus. Could the conference directorate actually safeguard the staff and participants? The issue of protection from infection went through several incarnations during the conference.

Once the conference started, one of the participants behaved like a "virus" himself, constantly attacking the thinking, interfering with the participants' ability to learn, and paralysing communication. The conference, titled "Between Inside and Outside: Navigating Authority and Leadership", dealt with issues of identity – interior and exterior – both in general and specific to each participant, with the pandemic looming in the background and highlighting these issues.

In retrospect, the dynamics of sibling relationships and the law of the mother can explain what happened at the conference. The "virus" participant represented the offending "sibling", and the group struggled to determine whether there was a "mother" to protect her other "children". The question that the participants and staff asked at the conference was whether the conference and its director could make sure that no one would harm anyone else. For example, in one of the groups, a participant ("X") said there was someone in the conference that X would like to have removed. The declaration stemmed from participant X's distress, but the staff report described a confrontation between the consultants about whether the director was protecting the participants and could ensure that X would not hurt anyone.

Slowly, it became clear that the staff and participants needed a statement of protection stating that no sibling would murder or hurt another sibling. We understand that unconsciously X was "sent" by the conference to announce that the law of the mother was in danger of collapse. This conduct in a group relations conference is extreme and comes as a reaction to the beginning of the pandemic, which, in itself, represents violence between siblings and the need for a guardian parent – the need for the law of mother.

A German–Israeli conference (PCCA)

German–Israeli Partners in Confronting Collective Atrocities (PCCA) is an organisation

> designed to provide opportunities for participants to explore how the full range of feelings and fantasies about "German-ness," "Israeli-ness," "Jewish-ness," "Palestinian-ness," and "Other-ness" influences relations within and between the different groups ... and how they affect and influence perceptions of the future.
>
> (PCCA, 2021)

The following example is taken from a PCCA conference in 2019.

Three consultants – two women and one man – were scheduled to participate in a large group in the conference. Normally, when a session is about to begin, two of the consultants are already seated, and the third, who is charged with timekeeping, closes the door. In this session, however, only one consultant was seated; just as the timekeeper was closing the door, the third consultant rushed in, and he and the timekeeper sat down together.

The session began with a story told by one of the German participants, the son of Nazi parents. The father had owned three special knives and a watch that were very important to him and had given these heirlooms to this son (the youngest one in the family). One day, the son (who perhaps felt guilty that his father had chosen him to keep the family treasures) decided to give the knives to his older brother. The older brother noticed that one of the knives bore a swastika and said that he wanted to remove the swastika from the knife. The younger brother objected fiercely. The older brother could not decide whether to have the swastika removed or not.

What was going on? The three consultants had come into the room in apparent disarray, an incident that suggested that something was awry among the consultants. The classic Oedipal, vertical axis-oriented interpretation would probably be that the three knives are the three consultants, whose interpretations are sometimes experienced by the participants as knife stabbings or as the cruel watch, which stops participants in mid-sentence at the end of the session.

On the horizontal axis, in terms of the sibling dynamics, we have a father who gave the things that were most precious to him to his youngest son, favouring him over his siblings. When the older brother finds out, the first thing he wants to do is erase this legacy, to erase the name of the father. The father failed to uphold the function of the law of the mother, which is not limited to the actual mother, in terms of maintaining and regulating intersibling dynamics. The father failed to handle the competition and hostility between the siblings, favouring the younger one over the older one. Hence, the knives can imply a "sabre dance" and a potential struggle between the sibling-members (Germans against Israelis, Israelis against Israelis, Germans against Germans, right-wingers against left-wingers in each nation, Eastern Europe against Western Europe, eastern Germany against western Germany, and so on). The watch might stand for the participants' wish to have someone there to protect them from a potential fratricide or incest between sibling-members. This interpretation does not favour one axis over the other but, rather, acts as an invitation to think about both axes – the vertical and the horizontal – as a way of obtaining a more complex and multidimensional picture of the overall dynamics.

Examples of the collapse of the law of the mother and its impact on Israeli society

The law of the mother as manifested in the position of the leader

In a press interview in 1976, which appears in the documentary film "Rabin: In His Own Words" (Laufer, as cited in the *Times* of Israel, 2015), the Israeli prime minister, Yitzhak Rabin, called the right-wing Gush Emunim movement, which was seeking to settle the occupied territories, "a cancer in the tissue of Israel's democratic society". The same Rabin who had once supported and aided the establishment of the settlements was now sowing the seeds of rupture in Israeli society.

With due caution, we would like to turn our attention to 1983, seven years after Rabin's statement, when Israel witnessed a fratricide stemming from ideological differences. Emil Grunzweig, an activist with a peace movement, was murdered during a rally when an Israeli right-wing demonstrator threw a grenade into the crowd.

Did Rabin's inflammatory words, which turned brother against brother, pave the way for, and legitimise, this murder? Did Rabin fail to uphold the law of the mother, an important responsibility of his role as the nation's leader? In 1995, Rabin himself was assassinated by an Israeli – one of the "sons". In the context of the law of the mother, the division in the country between the left and right wings led to a split between brothers and eventually to murder. It seems that Rabin was murdered by those brothers who felt that he had abandoned them, and they took revenge on him.

Sibling relationships and the law of the mother in the kibbutz

In the early days of the Zionist movement, kibbutzim were established based on the socialist doctrine of common ownership and equality and were run as shared communes. The cornerstone of the educational theory that the kibbutz movement created and applied was the minimisation of the negative effects of the Oedipal complex on the sexual investment of the parent (Liebermann, 2018; Rolnik, 2007). This investment was transferred to the group of sibling-children by having all children sleep in designated "children's houses", away from the bed of the parental couple. The nannies and the group of children were offered as alternative significant figures who would protect the child from Oedipal wishes and sexual impulses toward the parental couple. The group's siblings were perceived as safe figures, as a refuge from the perils of Oedipal wishes.

Sexuality was viewed only as directed at the parents, to the extent that, in addition to having the children sleep in a communal house rather than at home with their parents, the kibbutzim also created the custom of joint showers, with boys and girls showering together up to the age of eighteen. This practice sent young and adolescent boys and girls naked and exposed (both literally and figuratively) into a shared space, under the assumption that despite their hormone-struck age, the whole thing was merely "cubs at play".

The utter disregard for the significance of the horizontal axis as independently entailing sexuality, desire, and attraction and the excessive, potentially blinding focus on the Oedipal context of the vertical axis led to notions that we find completely absurd today. Moreover, we now know from the testimony of people who experienced this practice while growing up in a kibbutz that there were a great many physical and sexual assaults that were not reported or treated. The law of the mother had collapsed.

Bereaved siblings

Israel is known for its countless wars and resulting bereavement. Long ago, the country wisely established suitable institutions for addressing this issue. The state gives bereaved parents special help and emotional and financial support for the rest of their lives. Also, bereaved parents are always mentioned in Israel's Memorial Day services.

Until recently, however, bereaved siblings went unrecognised. Only in 2008 did Israel begin to acknowledge bereaved siblings as having been emotionally affected by the loss of their brother or sister; various state institutions finally started addressing the needs and rights of this segment of the population. The centrality of the Oedipal complex and parent–child relationships had no doubt influenced Israeli policy and its disregard for the bereavement suffered by siblings.

We might add that, by referencing only the child who was killed, the state failed in its role of the mother by neglecting to protect the surviving children.

Global example

The COVID-19 pandemic serves as an example of global "sibling" dynamics, exhibiting themes of comparison and competition for taking control of the virus and developing a vaccine for it while carrying out witch hunts to find culprits, infected people, and scapegoats. We view what happened in the world as a violation of the law of the mother, a failure to create order, cooperation, and responsibility among the siblings.

The competition over who will be the first to be vaccinated in general and who will give the third vaccine holds the desire to be the first and most special at the expense of others who are usually weaker than me compared to the possibility of cooperation and mutuality.

The law of the mother comes precisely to regulate such situations in which the competition for exclusivity is directed towards mutual cooperation and concern and that there is a place in the world not just for one.

A more positive enactment of the law of the father and of the mother can be seen in what is referred to as the traffic-light model in Israel (a similar system has been introduced in the European Union). Cities are classified as red, orange, yellow, or green according to their level of COVID-19 infection, and the pandemic regulations for their residents are based on the city's current colour. The model can be considered an integration of the law of the father, who sets the regulations, and the law of the mother, who says that not everyone is equal, but everyone will receive the appropriate treatment.

We suggest that the emerging presence of siblings in psychoanalytic discourse is likely related to the development of relational approaches that put the therapist–patient relationship and mutual influence at the centre of the therapeutic encounter. The horizontal connection in the therapeutic encounter, which also binds two subjects, constitutes, in our opinion, fertile ground for the development of approaches that speak of sibling relationships as affecting the growth of the inner world and the internalised image.

Conclusions

The horizontal relationship axis can be highly relevant to group work, group relations conferences, and society.

The unconscious phantasy (pre-concept) of being the one and only one in the whole universe and the narcissistic injury in the face of the recognition that it is not so, that we are one of a series, is of constitutive significance in our inner world and in our relationships with the other–siblings.

A group relationship workshop revives this vulnerability and constitutes an extensive cushion for the work and processing of the relationships that are re-enacted. The workshop staff, who work at the level of sibling relations in the team and as consultants in the various groups (participant siblings), have to hold both the horizontal axis and the vertical axis (authority levels) as having a decisive influence and crucial significance on the group and organisational interpersonal dynamics.

The connection between the vertical axis (Oedipal conflict) and the horizontal axis (sibling relationships) provides a complex, multidimensional view of personal, interpersonal, group, and organisational dynamics. We are not claiming that one axis is more influential than the other but, rather, that the matrix of the encounter between the two axes offers a deep, enriching picture of relationships.

References

Ashuach, S. & Talmi, S. (2022). The Law of the Mother and its expression in group relations conferences and organizations. In S. Ashuach & A. Berman (Eds), *Sibling Relations and the Horizontal Axis in Theory and Practice* (pp. 171–180). Abingdon, UK: Routlege.

Bion, W. (1961). *Experiences in Groups and Other Papers*. London: Tavistock

Freud, S. (1916–1917). *Introductory Lectures on Psycho-Analysis. The Standard Edition of the Complete Psychological Works of Sigmund Freud, XVI*: 241–463. London: Hogarth Press.

Freud, S. (1921c). *Group Psychology and the Analysis of the Ego. The Standard Edition of the Complete Psychological Works of Sigmund Freud, XVIII* (1920–1922). London: Hogarth Press.

Klein, M. (1952). Some theoretical conclusions regarding the emotional life of the infant. In P. Heimann, S. Isaacs, M. Klein, J. Riviere (Eds), *Developments in Psycho-Analysis* (Ch. 6). London: Hogarth.

Liebermann, G. (2018). *Freud in the Kibbutz: Psychoanalysis and Collective Education.* Jerusalem, Israel: Carmel.

Mitchell, J. (2003). *Siblings: Sex and Violence*. Cambridge: Polity.

Mitchell, J. (2006). Sibling trauma: a theoretical consideration. In P. Coles (Ed.) *Sibling Relationships* (pp. 155–174). London: Karnac.

Mitchell, J. (2018). Core Concepts: from sibling trauma to the law of the mother. Paper presented to the conference on siblings in individual and group. Psychoanalytic Psychotherapy. Tel Aviv University. Israel.

Partners in Confronting Collective Atrocities (PCCA) (2021). Our Conferences. The primary task of the recent conference. Available at http://p-cca.org/timeline/ (accessed 17 April, 2021).

Rolnik, E.J. (2007). *Freud in Zion. History of Psychoanalysis in Jewish Palestine/Israel 1918–1948*. Tel Aviv, Israel: Am Oved.

Part III

Post-conference Reflections

Introduction to Part III

Reflections on Belgirate VII

It is a tradition of the books emerging from the Belgirate meetings that in addition to the chapters that represent presentations that were made, participants are invited to write chapters reflecting on their experience. This year we have three remarkable chapters.

The first, "Behind the curtain of Belgirate VII: Reflections from the Tech Team", by Elyce Cole and Matt Gieve, offers insights into the (mostly) unseen but widely experienced work of the team that created and managed the virtual space for the meeting. They reflect on their work for, and interactions with, the Management and Administrative Team (MAT) as well as with the creator of QiqoChat, the software behind the virtual environment. They share their hypotheses about how their interactions with the MAT represented oscillating dependency dynamics (e.g., "between feeling like mere instruments (a pair of hands), lacking authorisation or not being invested with enough authority, to the other extreme ..."). They also reflect on the broader societal ambivalence about dependency on technology. Later in the chapter they consider technology and group relations as well as innovation and the future of GR.

Sivanie Shiran's chapter, "Our virtual footprint: Reflections on presence and absence," is at one level an account of her ambivalent participation as a presenter at Belgirate VII at a time when her husband was dealing with terminal cancer. She writes movingly about her hope that attending the virtual meeting would allow her "the prospect of joining the ranks of the living again, if only briefly." Her chapter is also about her experience of frustration with a virtual meeting: "The invitation to engage was genuine, but the means offered a poor substitute for the 'real deal'." She also describes a "rife sensorial imagery that burst forth on the outer boundaries of Belgirate VII" that she considers might "temptingly serve as a potent antidote to the isolation and discontinuous existence we experience online."

Finally, the editors are presenting a chapter that was not written as a reflective piece, but includes the authors' reflections on their interactions with the MAT from the time they made their initial Belgirate VII proposal to the end of the meeting. "Accepted and un-accepted", by Robert C Hsiung, Joseph E. Wise, and Jeffrey D. Roth, reports (from their perspective) having their presentation proposal for a "Trans-Language Continuous Online Group (TLCOG) for Belgirate VII" accepted

DOI: 10.4324/9781003502050-12

and then "unaccepted". They conducted the TLCOG outside the boundaries of Belgirate VII as the Cantina Across the Border. The chapter includes a history of the development of TLCOGs and the authors' extensive experience with asynchronous text-based groups. The second half of the chapter reflects on the possible psychodynamics of the "unacceptance" of the original proposal and what that might mean for a Belgirate orthodoxy. They also consider what they might represent to such an orthodoxy, including "step child", "illegitimate child", "mixed race child", "immigrant" and "illegal alien".

7

Behind the curtain of Belgirate VII

Reflections from the Tech Team

Elyce Cole and Matthew Gieve

Introduction

October 2021, as employees and representatives of the Tavistock Institute of Human Relations (TIHR), we were invited to take up the role of the "Tech Team" by the Management and Administrative Team (MAT) for the 7th convening of Belgirate, titled: "A Selfie: Portraying our Identity, Theory, and Practice". This chapter is our response to the conference title – a personal reflection and digestion of our experience in the role (of Tech Team) for Belgirate's first (and maybe only) virtual scientific meeting nearing the symbolic end of the Covid-19 pandemic.

First, we offer a reflexive narrative about what we (the Tech Team) noticed, felt and thought, and what it might symbolise/tell us about the angst/dilemma of society in a moment of great upheaval and technological advancement. Next, we make meaning of our experiences in the context of the group relations field's relationship to technology, given it is a methodology that first defined itself as a subversive technology in a different sense (Brissett, 2023). Included are themes that emerged around society's relationship to technology (dependency and authority) more broadly and, the field of group relations' relationship to innovation/change and its unknowable/unknown future (innovation, relevance and succession).

Methods used for data gathering and analysis: using MS Teams, we recorded ourselves for two unstructured virtual meetings that took place in January and February 2023, using the live transcription software. Next, we re-read the detailed verbatim transcript, highlighting salient themes, feelings, associations and hidden meanings between the text (thematic analysis). What follows are our insights/interpretations gleaned from the totality of this process. Unsurprisingly, our dialogue began with the question, "Where is the boundary?", which invites other related questions lurking beneath the surface: where are the boundaries in a virtual environment? What are the boundaries of this piece (i.e., how did we decide what to include or exclude)?

People in role

The role of the tech team was to develop and administer an online conference platform for nearly 100 participants via QiqoChat, a software "wrap" that allows

DOI: 10.4324/9781003502050-13

participants to move seamlessly from virtual room to virtual room (i.e., entering individual Zoom meetings). This task had two distinct parts, the pre-meeting phase characterised by the building of the wrap in collaboration with the software developer, and the in-meeting phase, characterised by the support of the participants, speakers and the MAT to navigate the various features of the platform. Although the main gathering space was online, the MAT still met in person, co-located at the head office of the TIHR in London, UK. Thus, we were, in effect, also managing a hybrid virtual experience/relationship between the MAT and participants. In sum, our role involved developing and maintaining the technological elements of the 7th convening of this scientific meeting. A further feature of the context of this role was that the development of a virtual conference occurred during a transitional year for the MAT; most members of the MAT were either new to the MAT or new to their role on the MAT. In addition, it was the MAT's first time working with a technology team.

While we, the authors, have some things in common – we are both neurodivergent millennials and senior consultants/researchers at the TIHR who studied psychoanalytic theory at postgraduate level. One a newer TIHR employee (just over three years) in conversation with an organisational veteran; an OD consultant debating with a social research evaluator; a Belgirate freshperson speaking to a returning participant; a cis-gender Black American bisexual middle-class woman collaborating with a cis-gender White British heterosexual middle-class man; a self-proclaimed group relations ambassador/advocate working alongside a perennial group relations sceptic. As the Tech Team, we make a dynamic pair. The following insights also reflect a dialogue between complementary/distinct parts of our professional and social selves.

As part of our forming stage in becoming a Tech Team, we talked through some of our fantasies and fears about taking up the role, and how it would be working together; we discussed the implications of our respective backgrounds and identities. Questions about seniority at the TIHR, considerations of nationality, culture, race, gender and our loyalty to the broader group relations framework all played a role in our conversations. We were acutely aware of the potential richness that could arise from these varied perspectives but also acknowledged the potential challenges in navigating them effectively. One prevalent concern was the fear of being perceived/treated as low-status or inexperienced, particularly considering the way group relations (and society in general) can undervalue, and sometimes infantilises, administrative support roles, especially when held by women or individuals of colour.

As we began, we found working together to be a dynamic and enlightening experience where our diverse perspectives and skills complemented one another, bringing a multifaceted approach to problem-solving and decision making, and allowing us to tackle complex tasks. We felt this process of pairing represented a commitment to inclusivity and a recognition of the value that diverse perspectives bring to the table. By working in this way, we were able to bridge gaps in understanding and create a more holistic approach to our shared responsibilities.

Inevitably, some of these fears came to life, some did not. However, we felt our collective commitment to open communication and mutual respect allowed us to navigate these challenges effectively.

Technology and society

Dependence and independence

A key theme to emerge from our discussions was around the way the introduction of new technology to the meeting had the potential to subvert traditional hierarchical relationships. While ostensibly in support roles, at times we felt overwhelmed by the MAT's dependency upon us, as gatekeepers of the technology, to make sense of the event's technological needs. While in matters of group relations and, in particular, the traditions of Belgirate, the MAT held greater experience, through the pre-meeting role we held a greater understanding of the functioning of the platform. This we felt created a persistent dynamic of us being invested with all technological competence (perhaps to the depletion of the MAT's own competence), sometimes manifesting itself with support requests not related to the platform but to other technologies (wifi, headphones, and so on). In relation to technology, therefore, we found ourselves in the position of "parenting the parents."

In parallel, we felt our own urgent dependence on the developer of QiqoChat in ways that were not always satisfied nor fulfilled. Instead of meeting our pleas for "just tell us how to do it/just do it for us", we were forced to be independent and make sense of an abundance of coding manuals. This challenged us to rise to the occasion, ultimately subverting traditional hierarchical relationships and fostering a deeper level of technical self-sufficiency.

Encountering challenges with the QiqoChat platform and its creator, as well as the MAT, elicited a sense of frustration within us. We grappled with their assumption that we could simply figure it out independently, which left us feeling somewhat abandoned and without the support we anticipated.

The pressure to possess all-encompassing knowledge was palpable and gave rise to metaphors such as Apple's Genius Bar or the enigmatic figure of the Wizard of Oz. We found ourselves in situations where we were expected to have all the answers, which created a weighty responsibility.

In these moments, we gained insight into the fragility of the entire system, recognising both the vulnerabilities of technology and the human element in its utilisation. It became evident that even the most sophisticated platforms can face hiccups, and our reliance on them is not without its potential pitfalls. As we navigated these challenges, we considered the identity of the "Wizard of Oz". Were we, the Tech Team, entrusted with this mantle, or was it the creator of QiqoChat?

This uncertainty sparked a desire to shift the onus of expertise and troubleshooting from the MAT to the Tech Team, and ultimately to the creator of QiqoChat. We sought a more balanced and collaborative approach, recognising that collective problem-solving could yield more effective and sustainable solutions.

Our experience in role supported the conclusion that technology can stir up a deep sense of dependency in all of us. The emergence of new technologies continually challenges and alters the nature and object of our dependence. At first, we considered the seeming contradiction between the dependence and independence it engenders. On the one hand, it acts as a facilitator for nearly every facet of our lives, extending and enhancing our capacities, to the extent that it is almost inconceivable to imagine living without. In the same breath, technology grants us a newfound level of independence and enables us to live more independently without constant intervention or assistance from fellow humans, enhancing our self-reliance. In this way, the taking up of new technologies could be seen as reducing or removing reliance on other people in exchange for increased reliance on technology. Shifting the object of dependence, not its existence.

In relation to communication technology particularly, we considered the way it simultaneously permits the creation of connections between individuals across vast distances, offering a promise of greater human contact. However, it can also inadvertently lead to feelings of isolation and loneliness. This paradox highlights the contrast between the contact technology enables and the detachment it can foster when individuals become immersed in their own virtual worlds. During the event, we witnessed these paradoxes unfold in tangible ways. The dynamic between dependence and independence was particularly evident.

Authority

As the Tech Team, we found ourselves grappling with a complex array of emotions and questions surrounding our authority and role within the larger context of the event. At times, we experienced a sense of uncertainty regarding the extent of our authority. In developing the platform, many decisions were needed that would have a substantive impact on the shape and participant experience of the meeting. We continually questioned whether we should "just make a call" or instead revert to the MAT for authorisation. This ambiguity led us to swing between feeling like mere instruments (a pair of hands), lacking authorisation or not being invested with enough authority, to the other extreme of feeling overly empowered (a pair of trousers), but hesitant to exercise this power.

Feeling de-authorised was a recurring theme, manifested in various ways. We often sensed a disconnect, with our input being ignored or overlooked. There were instances where we diligently undertook background work, only to find our suggestions met with a "yes, but" response from the MAT, leaving us to reconcile our efforts with their preferences. Moreover, when the MAT and the creator of Qiqo-Chat came together directly, we occasionally found ourselves feeling excluded and desiring to assume the role of intermediaries of technology. Were these incidents indicative of our initial fear about the status of administrative roles where the "backstage" work was not visible? At times we imagined ourselves serving as civil servants to a government, impartial and apolitical, enacting the MAT's desires rather than having the autonomy to shape the direction ourselves. This underscored the complexity of our authority and the intricate dance between the various stakeholders involved.

The challenge lay in developing a functioning organisational structure that included the addition of the virtual setting and the existence of the tech team. How could decisions be made in a timely way, especially when communication with the MAT was limited? We found ourselves wanting to be consultants to the MAT, offering insights and recommendations based on their discussions. However, at first, the tech team was not involved in MAT meetings and fed in separately. Without the necessary insight into their meetings, we often felt as if we were working in the dark, struggling to find our place in the larger framework. Once Belgirate VII had started, this led to interesting discussions about the position of the tech team in relation to the MAT; were we part of the MAT, a subgroup for example, or something separate with a discreet function?

As the meeting progressed, we were increasingly brought into MAT discussions allowing for this two-way dialogue. Reflecting afterwards, we wondered whether the initial omission of the tech team from these spaces related to the novel (virtual) setting of the meeting and the novel role of the tech team, or whether it represented unconscious beliefs about the role of technology, as a purely technical servant. Developing this thought, we questioned whether this belief is justified, whether technology was subordinate to human beings, serving us as masters, or if, in fact, we were becoming increasingly subservient to technology. This introspection led to a deeper understanding of the power dynamics at play, leading us to consider the potential subversive role of technology in reshaping traditional hierarchies. In moments of pressure and urgency, we couldn't help but draw parallels to the expectation that we should possess all the answers, akin to the omniscient Siri. This perspective, while acknowledging the power of technology, also highlighted the need for human input to truly bring it to life.

Ultimately, our role as the Tech Team was a nuanced one, situated somewhere in-between, tasked with bridging the gap between the MAT and QiqoChat. We found ourselves navigating a delicate balance between being the polyglots, translators and interpreters of both group relations and technology. This role, while challenging, held a certain power in subverting traditional hierarchies and providing essential support to the larger endeavour.

Technology and group relations

Our experience of the dynamics between the Tech Team and the MAT highlighted the following themes: ambivalence towards technology and resistance to change; technology-backed omnipotence, and competition between tradition and innovation.

Ambivalence towards technology and resistance to change

The data: The MAT waited to engage us (the Tech Team) at the last minute and repeatedly expressed disappointment that Belgirate VII could not be in person.

What we felt: As result, we often felt "as if" we were operating without a clear roadmap, because we were unaware of the MAT's vision/criteria and aware that we were all navigating unchartered territory.

Our interpretation: Did our experience reflect a potential ambivalence within the MAT towards technology and resistance to/sabotage of change.

Technology-backed omnipotence

The data: Designing our digital landscape using QiqoChat required us to have an opinion on an exhaustive list of settings. If we had not gone through this process, our conference rooms would effectively cease to exist. That is, we had to build our digital environment, which differs slightly from an in-person environment. Although one still needs to decide how to arrange the room, the room itself still persists regardless of occupancy.

What we felt: As a result, we were in touch with a heightened sense of omnipotence and competence because of the power we had to shape most aspects of our virtual environment.

Our interpretation: Although we experienced a sense of omnipotence as Belgirate's "digital creators", we later considered that our experience of omnipotence concealed a degree of denial about our dependence on either the MAT or the legacy of GR and its esteemed predecessors. A further reflection hypothesised that maybe we too were ambivalent about our perceived power as a Tech Team and were hesitant to challenge/upstage our elders.

Competition between tradition and innovation

The data: There was an incident where a member of the Tech Team felt they had inadvertently dismissed an outgoing member of the MAT.

What we felt: There was an unspoken competition between the Tech Team and the MAT to provide containment for the participants of Belgirate VII.

Our interpretation: This unspoken competition mirrored the tension/competition between virtual and in-person group relations conferences. The MAT perhaps represented established norms, practices and technology, while we represented a newer approach.

Our interpretation of our experience in relation to the wider field of group relations

We felt our experience mirrored a broader ambivalence in the field of GR towards virtual modes of operation and noticed (or at least perceived) a hierarchy in the mind that placed in-person GR practice above virtual GR practice. We speculated if perhaps the competition between in-person GR practice and technology-enabled GR practice is because the GR community considers GR itself to be a type of technology and therefore is reluctant to compete with newer, digital methods of engagement. How the GR community chooses to embrace virtual space is crucial to its survival and ability to remain relevant for the future of work. The GR community must acknowledge that virtual GRCs are not just a shallow imitation of face-to-face GRCs but, in fact, a new location to study the particularities of virtual group behaviour that mirrors the virtual working world. As society increasingly conducts itself virtually, generating understanding and insights into the features of online ways of working remains crucial.

We wondered how our experience reflected the field's broader apprehension and anxiety about staying current, perhaps fearing obsolescence in the face of advancing technology, practices and other ways of knowing. Again, this mirrors the wider concerns of psychodynamic disciplines' anxieties about "being left behind" but also wishing to sustain the valuable practices and insights from earlier generations. That is, how to innovate and build on the wisdom of past traditions.

Our preceding reflections illuminate the implicit intergenerational tensions that arise within the evolving landscape of technology and GR and the need for open dialogue and mutual understanding. Further, these reflections prompted us to consider whether these different forms of engagement are really in competition, or if they can coexist harmoniously.

Conclusion: The future of GR

In reflecting upon our journey as the Tech Team for the 7th convening of Belgirate, we find ourselves immersed in a tapestry of experiences, perspectives and challenges that signal something meaningful for the future of GR re: innovation, societal relevance and succession planning. The attempted, one-off virtual migration of an ongoing series of in-person meetings, and our role in holding the technological element of this, furnished us with a kind of test-bed to experience many pervasive tensions of the GR field amid an increasingly fluid, networked and virtual world.

The need for innovation

One of the key drivers of change in the field is innovation, and while we know innovative GR practices exist and continue to emerge, it raises an important question about how the GR community embraces innovation (e.g., novel events, different formats and settings, and topics and applications) and how such innovations are incorporated into standard practice. In this evolving landscape, it is crucial to acknowledge those underrepresented in the field. Among them are GR practitioners and members of colour, whose contributions and unique insights are sometimes met with resistance; non-binary and trans GR practitioners and members who are overlooked by outdated modes of interpreting group behaviour; and GR practitioners and members who are newer to the work and excluded due to the financial costs, time constraints and limited access to affordable trainings and conferences.

Societal relevance

This brings us to a fundamental question: is GR primarily a form of play, or is it intrinsically linked to the larger task of understanding and influencing the world? The relevance of GR and its fit for purpose are a topic of ongoing discussion. It's noteworthy that, in our discussion thus far, we tended to introduce the concept of members later, a tendency we associate with the insular nature of GR. This introspective focus, while valuable for self-reflection, prompts us to consider how it aligns with the broader needs of the world. One pressing concern revolves around the anxiety surrounding the future health and continuity of the GR method, particularly in the absence of a clear succession plan. This raises the imperative of revising the method to ensure its continued pertinence and efficacy in evolving contexts. The irony of a central insight from group relation's theoretical underpinning, open systems theory, is that systems must adapt to the environment to survive.

Intergenerational dynamics and succession planning

Whether it is the boomers, bloomers or those in between, the notion of agelessness emerges, highlighting the diversity of concerns and aspirations that shape the field's trajectory. Additionally, there exists a palpable ambivalence among inheritors of the GR tradition, who may grapple with a sense of duty towards a method that holds deep familial significance. The challenge lies in reconciling this inherited legacy with their personal passions and commitments, as they navigate their unique relationship with the field.

The poem "Self-portrait at 28", by David Berman, encapsulates the essence of our paired experiences – a continuous evolution, a willingness to adapt, and an openness to transformation. Our journey as the Tech Team for Belgirate's virtual scientific meeting has been a profound sociotechnical exploration of the intersection of technology, GR, and what it means to evolve.

Reference

Brissett, L.B. (2023, 14 February). Group relations: A thought piece. Tavistock Institute of Human Relations. Available at https://tavinstitute.org/news/group-relations-gnostic-reticularity-and-the-politics-of-revelation

8

Our virtual footprint

Reflections on presence and absence

Sivanie Shiran

My husband was dying. That much was made clear in September 2020, when the doctor revealed to us that what appeared to be a midlife backache was actually terminal Stage IV pancreatic cancer.

The effect of this pronouncement had been to call me to attention. Like a soldier called to battle, I jolted to full alert. Everything around me fell immediately into razor focus: nothing could be taken for granted any more; everything counted; how we used time *mattered*. Caring for my husband as he attended weekly chemotherapy and battled the advancing illness filled me with a clear sense of purpose. Loving well seemed the only worthy goal left standing. I couldn't be bothered any more with half-lies and self-deceptions. It was clear now that they were too costly and that I could no longer afford them. One of the telltale signs of real living is the bearing of crisp, unflinching truth. In this sense, I had never felt more alive.

Our life quickly filled with doctors' appointments, day-long chemotherapy sessions, and CT scans. Time became punctuated by varied medications, all intended to manage the increasing side-effects of the so-called "treatment". We valiantly struggled to keep our moods up, knowing that this was the battleground on which all would be lost or won. But what our attitudes belied, our clothing revealed, and soon we found that we had casually slipped into wearing our pyjamas for most of the day. A degree of self-loathing inevitably crept up on me as death and illness seemed to infuse every molecule of the air we breathed. We had become a world unto ourselves.

So when the call to register for the online Belgirate conference arrived in my inbox, it brought with it a fresh whiff of the world "out there" and the promise of re-engaging with "real life". As the day approached, I became excited at the prospect of joining the ranks of the living again, if only briefly.

I indulged the idea of taking the time to attend Belgirate VII with the flimsy excuse that I would present the work we did on the global eGRC at the outset of the pandemic. The conference staff group had asked me to speak on our behalf at the panel for virtual GRCs and though I had tried to wriggle my way out of it, I ultimately felt somewhat duty-bound. Presence at Belgirate VII, it seemed, was going to necessitate being seen.

DOI: 10.4324/9781003502050-14

But as I shuffled to put myself in some semblance of order, the messages started pouring in. Two staff members would be unable to attend – one because they were caring for a small child, the other because they were expecting the birth of a grandchild. And just as Belgirate VII launched, I too was called away to go buy more morphine for my husband. *Arriving* at the online version of Belgirate – let alone being *present* there – was already proving to be challenging.

When I flipped on my computer screen, it was not long before I lost interest altogether. The excitement at the prospect of healthy discourse was soon replaced with an aching disappointment reminiscent of having to use a condom in bed. The invitation to engage was genuine, but the means offered a poor substitute for the "real deal".

I found myself renegotiating my personal contract with the organisation in my mind. The new, unconscious contract, went something like this: if I was to be denied intimacy and relegated to a more passive, unseen position, I would avenge myself by denying the organisation my attentive gaze. As I listened to the speeches unfold in plenary, I found myself quickly "checking out", sneaking peeks at other realms of my life, like a bandit that could never be caught because the escape route lay just beyond the Zoom frame. I was reminded of the insight offered by D.W. Winnicott (1984) in which he framed delinquent acts as a form of entitlement, a Robin Hood claim to right what was unjustly withheld in childhood.

But rather than feeling righteous, I felt duped. My unforeseen punishment was to find myself precisely in the place I had hoped to avoid. "Checked out" and "unseen", I felt increasingly dead at Belgirate VII. Although I had registered for the conference in the hope of "coming alive", my feelings went flat, and you could hardly discern a clinical heartbeat as I listened to the lectures. It would not be long before I yearned to go back to my husband, illness and all.

The absence of a full-bodied opportunity to connect at Belgirate VII had inadvertently stirred in me another layer of loss. At first, I concentrated intensely, vigilantly scanning the landscape of the little tiles on my screen to try to glean hints of what was hidden, yet present. Then I leaned in, struggling harder to enter, like a frustrated lover whose hunger is fed by the inaccessible proximity of her object. But the harder I tried, the more I failed to take in the full mosaic that lay before me.

Perhaps the lines between the computer screen and myself had temporarily blurred, the container inevitably affecting the contained. Perhaps my deadness reflected a sort of participation mystique[1] with the cold, inanimate technology we were inhabiting.

Or perhaps the loss of a full-bodied connection online was simply one too many losses for me to bear. Simon Western (2022), in his article "Presence and absence: Melancholia and confusion in the digital age", notes that it is the cyclical dance between presence and absence that takes place online that renders our experience of loss particularly acute. He poignantly notes the paradox that although our live presence on the screen may offer comfort/joy, at the same time it accentuates our experience of loss by reminding us that we are in fact apart. Maybe, rather than contending with the grief at Belgirate, I "played dead", muting my mind and my voice, while hiding in plain view.

The deprivation of touch and smell online seemed to aggravate an old wound. The primal need for attachment through physical proximity (Bowlby, 1969) re-opened and still longed to be filled, like the lost maternal experience of infancy or the nostalgic ache for "home". In the global eGRC we had organised during the pandemic, loss of intimacy and a longing for closeness to the authority figures were indeed among the prominent themes that emerged. This gaping primal attachment need had been partially fulfilled by the conference administrator, whose role I likened to the blind guide who had once led me through a pitch-black exhibit hall. My transference to the guide had been one of overwhelming dependency and gratitude, as I relished in the attunement and compassion she rained down on me, my temporary blindness heightening my experience of feeling seen.

During Belgirate VII, I too found my way unconsciously to the administrator's room – hoping perhaps for a deeper connection than was possible elsewhere. Slowly, as I sat amid the cold and inanimate context, a torrent of compensatory associations rife with sensorial imagery began to emerge. As Belgirate unfolded online, the group WhatsApp of our eGRC conference staff began dinging loudly outside of the conference sphere. Efferent pictures of breastfeeding newborn babies came pouring in, the warmth of the evocative exchanges contrasting starkly with the remote communications emanating from our screens. It was as though the unacknowledged absence of olfactory and tactile connections at the virtual conference was being compensated for by a swelling of eros connections in the under-seam of the conference realm. The longing for greater intimacy that hung in the air was expressed most poignantly perhaps by one of the conference staff members who recounted being mesmerised by my lips while I presented on the virtual panel online. The yearning for eros was palpable.

In the discussion that followed the panel on virtual GRCs at Belgirate VII, I too found myself wondering aloud how a GRC might be different if housed in the ecosystem of a rain forest as opposed to a computer network. The question belied a yearning for a more luscious experience – one coursing with vitality and the mysteries of nature.

This yearning was reminiscent of a process quietly referred to in the grief literature as "erotic mourning". It refers to an acute sexual longing sometimes experienced by mourners after the loss of a loved one. Irvin Yalom (2021) spoke of it bravely in his book *A Matter of Death and Life*, in which he described the erotic fantasies that inundated him after his wife passed away from a terminal illness. Absence mixed with imagination may indeed be the mortar of eroticism (Perel, 2013).

But it is not merely, or even primarily, a sexual longing that is awakened by the loss of profound connection, but rather a heightened sensuality. A feeling that in the wake of death, life is more vivid, more intense, has often been reported by war-weary soldiers, Holocaust survivors, and doctors encountering terminal patients. It is as though these cutting confrontations with death force us "to break open", removing, if only temporarily, the mental barrier that separates, so clearly and artificially, between ourselves and others, between ourselves and life.

It is the poetry of the erotic attitude that seems to lure us back from the edge to the sensuous textuality of life, tethering our souls to the world of the living, to the here and now. Perhaps the rife sensorial imagery that burst forth on the outer boundaries of Belgirate VII was a way of contending with the mortality of our physical selves online. In a virtual world where our material presence seems no longer to *matter* at all, perhaps we develop a thirst for drinking life in through our senses. In this context, the erotic sensibility temptingly serves as a potent antidote to the isolation and discontinuous existence we experience online[2].

I had fled to Belgirate VII to avoid facing my husband's imminent death and my impending loss, but other than the panel on virtual GRCs, I was AWOL for most of the conference sessions because I couldn't bear the feeling of deadness online. But even as I absented myself from Belgirate, Belgirate remained present in me. I wondered in the back of my mind what it actually meant to be *present*, what it means to "*show up*". The question on my mind wasn't so much about the impact of the virtual world on our lives, but rather what it means to be fully, versus virtually, present in *life* – what it means to be *living*.

My husband was dying, yes, but so was I. So are we all, in fact, from the day we are born. So, we are living *and* dying every day of our lives. Coming alive is a choice. And not an easy one. It means showing up and devoting ourselves to something real. Even as we try our hardest not to make a mess, we cannot avoid the undeniable fact that to be present inherently means to cast a shadow as well.[3]

In an interview Maya Angelou gave to *The Paris Review* in the autumn of 1990, she poignantly noted:

> Most people don't grow up. It's too damn difficult. What happens is most people get older. That's the truth of it. They honor their credit cards, they find parking spaces, they marry, they have the nerve to have children, but they don't grow up. Not really. They get older. But to grow up costs the earth, the earth. It means you take responsibility for the time you take up, for the space you occupy. It's serious business. And you find out what it costs us to love and to lose, to dare and to fail. And maybe even more, to succeed. What it costs, in truth. Not in superficial costs – anybody can have that – I mean in truth.

I wondered to myself whether attending Belgirate VII online had been a worthy choice. I seemed to be going through the motions. Waiting for something clever to be said, or for something unpredictable to reveal itself. But I didn't really show up. Not really.

But, as Belgirate VII drew to a close, feeling somewhat ashamed and self-deprived, I participated in what was intended to be a debrief session of the experience. Inspired by the heavyweights in my small group and a mourner's sense of "who gives a shit?", I decided to take a leap of faith and speak my truth. Hence, I shared with my fellow sojourners that in most of the sessions I had attended I had resisted sharing what I truly thought because I feared that if I did, the only conference I would ever be invited to staff would be Belgirate in three years' time. This utterance seemed to usher in a collective sigh of relief. Someone had finally said the unsayable and had lived to tell. Courage, it seems, is both a prerequisite and a product of coming alive.

Finally, as Belgirate concluded and the pixels on my screen evaporated, the ephemerality of our existence was poignantly brought home to me.

Confucius famously said, "We have two lives, and the second begins when we realise we only have one".

Inner authority is uncaged when we agree to pay the price for showing up to it.

Notes

1 Borrowing from Levy-Bruhl (1910), C.G. Jung described "participation mystique" as follows:

> … a peculiar kind of psychological connection with objects, and consists in the fact that the subject cannot clearly distinguish himself from the object but is bound to it by a direct relationship which amounts to partial identity (q.v.). This identity results from an a priori oneness of subject and object. Participation mystique is a vestige of this primitive connection.
>
> (Jung, 1971)

2 The French philosopher, Georges Bataille (1962), defined eroticism as a transgression from our discontinuous existence as isolated beings, into an experience of continuous existence.

3 C.G. Jung employs the metaphor of the shadow to denote those aspects of our psyche that lie in our personal unconscious – hidden or unconscious aspects of oneself, both good and bad, which the ego has either repressed or never recognised (Jung, 1969).

References

Angelou, M. (1990). The art of fiction (interview). *The Paris Review, 116.*

Bataille, G. (1962). *Death & Sensuality: Study of Eroticism and the Taboo.* New York: Walker. Originally published *as L'Erotisme* (1957). Paris: Les Editions de Minuit.

Bowlby, J. (1969). *Attachment and Loss, Vol. 1: Attachment.* New York: Basic Books.

Jung, C.G. (1969). Aion: Researches into the phenomenology of the self (R.F.C. Hull, Trans.). In H. Read et al. (Eds), *The Collected Works of C.G. Jung*: *Vol. 9* pt. 2, par. 14. Princeton, NJ: Princeton University Press.

Jung, C.G. (1971). Psychological types. *Collected Works, Vol 6,* par. 781. Princeton, NJ: Princeton University Press.

Levy-Bruhl, L. (1910). *Les fonctions mentales dans les societies inferieures*, translated (1926) from French as *How Natives Think.* London: G. Allen & Unwin, 1910.

Perel, E. (2013). The secret to desire in a long-term relationship (video). TED Talk. Available at https://www.youtube.com/watch?v=sa0RUmGTCYY

Western, S. (2022). Presence and Absence: Melancholia and confusion in the digital age, Kav Ofek (2), online publication.

Winnicott, D. W. (1984). *Deprivation and Delinquency*. London: Tavistock.

Yalom, I. & Yalom, M. (2021). *A Matter of Death and Life*. Redwood Press.

9

Accepted and un-accepted

Robert C. Hsiung, Joseph E. Wise, and Jeffrey D. Roth

Introduction

We proposed a Trans-Language Continuous Online Group (TLCOG) for Belgirate VII. The Management and Administrative Team (MAT) accepted our proposal. The MAT then un-accepted it. We reimagined it and proceeded with it outside the Belgirate boundary as the Cantina Across the Border. The theme of Belgirate VII was "Group Relations 2021: A Selfie Portraying Our Identity, Theory, & Practice" (Belgirate VII Brochure). Did the TLCOG hold something that could not be fully accepted into the frame of the Belgirate VII selfie?

(We use "unaccepted" here in its usual sense, "not accepted", and "un-accepted" to mean a reversal/undoing of accepted.)

The Trans-Language Continuous Online Group

A Continuous Online Group (COG) is a text-based online large group that stays open "24/7" for two weeks. Members interact "asynchronously" (not in "real" time) by e-mail or on a website.

Hsiung and Roth with various colleagues have offered a COG in conjunction with the annual meeting of the American Group Psychotherapy Association (AGPA) every year since 2007 (Storck, 2007), the international symposium of the Group Analytic Society international in 2014 and 2017, the national conference of the South African Psychoanalytic Confederation in 2016, and the AKRI Dialogues in 2019. Wise took a member role in the AGPA COG for five years and joined the COG team in 2019. Others have transitioned in the other direction, from staff roles to member roles.

An asynchronous text-based online group is more accessible than a synchronous online group or an in-person group. Participants can be anywhere in the world, so they do not have to travel. A COG can "hold" an in-person conference, providing space to warm up before, to process during, and to debrief after. Time zones are not an obstacle, and there are no schedule conflicts with other meeting activities. A transcript allows members to "rewind". Text can be easier to understand than speech, especially for those who are not native speakers.

A COG is radically accessible. A member once flew to an in-person meeting and posted to the COG from baggage claim. A COG is not a group that members go to

DOI: 10.4324/9781003502050-15

when and where the staff schedule it. A COG is a group that members carry around in their pocket and attend whenever they choose.

A COG is not a group relations conference and has never been part of one. Clearly, its boundaries differ from those of traditional group relations events.

A web page interface can allow alternative views of a COG. A "subgroup view" displays posts separated by discussion "thread" (topic). A "group-as-a-whole view" displays posts in a single chronological list.

A TLCOG is a COG with built-in translation. Integration with Google Translate makes a TLCOG accessible to those who read and write any of 104 languages (Google Cloud). "Machine translation" is an "assistive device" for communication, like a wheelchair is for mobility.

Machine translation is imperfect, but can be good enough. At an online conference offered by Group Relations India, a member posted something in English in the chat, someone who had not been speaking much English asked for translation, Hsiung posted a Google Translation, and someone later told him they were surprised how good his Hindi was.

Consider also one's self-accessibility. Our hypothesis was that engaging in one's mother tongue would increase access to one's "child self", one's less professional and more regressed parts.

Accepted and un-accepted

We submitted a proposal for a TLCOG at Belgirate VII. It included the timing of the phases of the TLCOG:

> The TLCOG is a COG that uses machine translation to enable members with any of 104 native languages to "speak" (post) in their mother tongues and to be "heard" (read) by others in the others' native languages. The TLCOG opens before and closes after the events in Olhão and consists of four phases: orientation Oct 23–25, experiential Oct 25–Nov 3, review and application Nov 3-–5, and departure Nov 5–6 (all 2021). Participating in the TLCOG does not preclude participating in any other Belgirate event. Nor does it require going to Olhão.

The Management and Administrative Team (MAT) accepted our proposal. The MAT then un-accepted it. We reacted with shock, confusion, anger and sadness. The MAT was open to looking at this process and allowed us to remain on the Virtual Group Relations Conference Panel. The MAT also offered us the alternative of a parallel presentation. We opted to remain on the Panel. This process was repeated when we asked to add a colleague to the TLCOG team, the MAT accepted them, and the MAT then un-accepted them.

The Cantina Across the Border

We did not want to abandon the TLCOG, so we reimagined it as the Cantina Across the Border an open, asynchronous, text-based, 104-language online experience outside the Belgirate VII boundary. We invited those at Belgirate VII to venture outside the boundary, and we invited those not at Belgirate VII to come to the boundary.

"Cantina" was a reference to the hangout at which multiple languages were spoken in Mos Eisley, on Tatooine, in the film *Star Wars*. "Across the Border" alluded to the boundary between the US and Mexico.

The Cantina opened on 21 October, 2021 and closed on 12 November, 2021. On the website, posts could be translated by clicking a button. Posts automatically translated and sent by e-mail included the message in both the original and translated languages.

117 messages were posted by 15 visitors (including Hsiung and Wise). Nine of those messages were posted in languages other than English.

Reflections: The Belgirate in the mind

Our proposal, though clearly for a group, was misunderstood as a proposal for a presentation. We hypothesise that "the Belgirate in the mind", in which all proposals are for presentations, was activated and precluded understanding what our proposal was actually for.

When translating, what one person says is not what the other person hears. When something is expressed, but not understood, it is "lost in translation". That our proposal was for a group (with translation) was ironically lost in translation.

The stated criterion for eligibility to attend Belgirate was having "held a staff role" (Belgirate VII Brochure). Our colleague had held a consultant role, but as a member of the training subgroup of a member group. In "the Belgirate in the mind", eligibility derived from having been a member of a staff group. Group affiliation trumped experience (and the stated criterion).

"The Belgirate in the mind", like most conferences, was binary. The events were for the group relations "family" (Belgirate VII Brochure) and not for others. There was interest in both points of view: "What do we see? What would a 'tourist' see?" (Belgirate VII Brochure), but no provision for tourists, let alone learning what they saw. The Cantina Across the Border, to which both participants and non-participants were invited, presented a non-binary alternative.

Varieties of acceptance and unacceptance

A number of metaphors illustrate varieties of acceptance and unacceptance in the context of a family.

Mixed-race child

The COG is mixed-race in the sense that it is the "child" of "parents" of disparate cultures. Roth "grew up" in the culture of group relations. He directed his first group relations conference in 2002. The COG is the younger sibling of Psycho-Babble

(Hsiung, 2000; Heffernan, 2010), an online peer support group example of "Web 2.0" established by Hsiung in 1988, the year before that term was coined (Wikipedia), as an application of the Internet to mental health (Hsiung, 2002).

One focus of group relations is on authority (Green & Molenkamp, 2005) in the sense of "conferred power to perform a service" (Heifetz, 1994). Another is on the "here-and-now" (Hayden & Molenkamp, 2002). Web 1.0 became Web 2.0 when "users" who previously had only the role of consuming/receiving "content" became empowered to produce content and to interact with each other. That empowerment was authorisation conferred not by another person, group, or organisation, but by software. Web 2.0 was, and now "social media" is, largely asynchronous. Asynchronous processes call into question where is "here" and when is "now".

Hsiung was open to group relations, having attended his first group relations conferences in 1987 and 1988, and Roth was open to Web 2.0. Having noticed the emergence of "chat rooms" dedicated to recovery from addiction in the late 1990s, he became interested in the group and organisational dynamics of virtual groups. He directed the first virtual group relations conference, using an online "bulletin board" in an asynchronous mode, in 2006 (Roth, 2007; Lipgar, 2007; Behal 2009, 2016).

Roth also studied the group and organisational dynamics of virtual Al-Anon groups, mutual support groups for the families and friends of problem drinkers (Roth & Tan, 2007, 2008). He published other early work on group relations in cyberspace in Kav Ofek (Roth, 2008) and *Psychoanalytic Inquiry* (Kohn & Roth, 2012). He directed Virtual Large Study Groups with an international staff from five sponsoring organisations on an online bulletin board in 2009 and 2010.

With much of the world sheltering in place in the spring of 2020, the resulting physical isolation (Na et al., 2022) created both challenges and opportunities for group relations work. Roth directed one of the first virtual group relations conferences on Zoom, for psychiatric chief residents, that August, and a second virtual GRC, for Chinese members, that December. A third, for Russian-speaking members, followed in March, 2021, and a fourth, again for psychiatrists in training, in May, 2021.

Illegitimate child

The Belgirate VII brochure referred to the group relations "family". The Tavistock Institute of Human Relations could be considered the parent, OFEK (the Israeli Association for the Study of Group and Organizational Processes) and AKRI (the A. K. Rice Institute) its children. At a family's boundary of acceptance and unacceptance are illegitimate children. Their genetics are impure: half legitimised by marriage, half not. The TLCOG may have had a valence for illegitimacy. One member of its team was a certified AKRI consultant (A. K. Rice Institute), but none of the others had been so legitimised.

Stepchild

In between a legitimate child and an illegitimate child is a stepchild (the non-literal meaning of which is "one that fails to receive proper care or attention"). The American/AKRI members of the TLCOG team did have the wish that the American/AKRI members of the MAT would advocate for them/the TLCOG.

Illegal alien

At a country's boundary of acceptance and unacceptance are illegal aliens. "Cantina Across the Border" alluded to the boundary between the US and Mexico. There, a physical wall and policies like Remain in Mexico (Wikipedia) kept the doubly unacceptable (not only alien, but also illegal) out of the US. "The U.S.-Mexican border es una herida abierta [is an open wound] where the third world grates against the first and bleeds" (Anzaldua, 1987).

Acceptance and un-acceptance can both be in the service of purity, and nationalism, a wish for solidarity based on a single identity, was on the rise.

Immigrant

An immigrant not only can contribute to "brain drain" from their old country, but also can experience "brain waste" (underemployment) in their new country. If their credentials are not recognised, they cannot put their skills to use. Surgeons come to the US and drive taxis. Similarly, the TLCOG team was allowed to enter Belgirate VII, and were offered "jobs" (the opportunity to give a parallel presentation), but could not "ply their trade". The TLCOG team held feelings of rejection, hurt, aggrievement, anger and grief.

Mutation

COVID-19 forced Belgirate VII from Olhão to Zoom. The "China virus" (Venditto, 2020) sparked anti-Asian hate. Both could have contributed to Belgirate VII closing its border to a proposal for an event that may have been perceived as a mutation from a team led by a Chinese American.

Siblings

The TLCOG has a "sibling", the Trans-Modal COG, or TMCOG, which embraces different modalities (asynchronous text and synchronous video and in-person) rather than different languages. Belgirate, in Europe, could be considered to have a "child", the AKRI Dialogues, in the US. A TMCOG crossed the AKRI Dialogues boundary in 2019, yet a TLCOG could not cross the Belgirate boundary in 2022.

The TMCOG may have been experienced by the AKRI Dialogues as more "us" and the TLCOG by Belgirate VII as more "them". The AKRI Dialogues used to meet in Chicago, home to both Hsiung and Roth. Hsiung lived literally next door to the retreat and conference centre at which the Dialogues were held.

An entrepreneur mindset is more common and comfort with competition is greater in the US than in Europe (Manchin, 2010). The US may be an earlier adopter of innovation (Rogers, 1962), which could have been a factor in the AKRI Dialogues adopting a TMCOG and Belgirate VII not adopting a TLCOG.

Different modalities may have been experienced as acceptable while different languages may have been experienced as unacceptable. There may have been interest in online modalities, which may have been seen as a "growth edge", especially in the US, while other languages may have threatened the dominance of English (Berthoud et al., 2023) and the privilege of being able to speak English, and, indirectly, white supremacy, and, more generally, the supremacy of "the way it is".

The incorporation of translation into group relations conferences is an innovation that has led to a new category of staff member, translator/cultural interpreter, and a new role for software (Trans-Language Continuous Online Group, 2017; China and the World GRC in 2022; Ball, 2022). Distortions can, however, be introduced by both the lack of immediacy and by the limitations of meaningful translation of nuanced associations (Harkins et al., 2021).

The International Cohort Group of AKRI (A. K. Rice Institute) convenes meetings which are in part also non-binary in that participants and non-participants of group relations conferences discuss them together (after the conferences). Wise, as a participant in a group relations conference, has, during it, invited discussion in the Tavistock Community (Wise, 2023) with non-participants.

Ambivalence

The TLCOG was not simply unaccepted; it was accepted and then un-accepted. That could have reflected ambivalence. Saying "yes" can be a slip of the tongue. What the unconscious desires can be unacceptable to the ego, also known as management and administration. Alternatively, one's eyes can be bigger than one's stomach. The spirit can be willing, but the flesh weak.

The global group relations family may have been struggling with ambivalence about working online. The validity, value and relevance of group relations in the virtual space was tested as a result of the COVID-19 pandemic.

Conclusions

We did submit our proposal for a group despite the Call for Papers (Belgirate VII Call for Papers) calling for parallel presentations. It may be that we were used by the system to clarify limits and to model the conflict between authorising oneself and conforming to the group, the "scapegoat leader" role (Beck et aal., 1989).

Systems cannot take in/close their boundaries to differences that are too great (Agazarian et al., 2020), even if that which is different may be helpful or tasty. The TLCOG may have been too different to be taken in by Belgirate VII. The TLCOG team may have held, and enacted, "otherness".

Too different can also mean too early (Gobry, 2011). Perhaps in a future generation, a group relations conference (either in-person or online) will have a

Continuous Online Event. The COE could open up learning about asynchronous group relations and be a legitimate member of the group relations 'family'.

This is our "selfie" at Belgirate VII.

References

Agazarian, Y.M., Gantt, S.P. & Carter, F.B. (2020). *Systems-Centered Training.* Routledge.

A. K. Rice Institute for the Study of Social Systems. Certified Consultants of the A. K. Rice Institute. https://www.akriceinstitute.org/certified-consultants

Anzaldua, G. (1987). *Borderlands/La Frontera: The New Mestiza.* San Francisco, CA: Spinster/Aunt Lute Press.

Ball, D. (2022, 24 August). Bridge the language gap and connect people with Zoom translated captions. Zoom Blog. Available at https://blog.zoom.us/translated-captions

Beck, A.P., Eng, A.M. & Brusa, J.A. (1989 Fall/Winter). The evolution of leadership during group development. *Group, 13*(3 & 4).

Behal, A. (2009). Echoes from the staff room. Available at https://app.box.com/s/zl8g1skusn/file/328609952

Behal, A. (2016). Lure of the unknown: First online conference in the Tavistock tradition. Available at https://www.academia.edu/29368111/Lure_of_the_Unknown_First_Online_Conference_in_the_Tavistock_Tradition

Belgirate VII Brochure. Available at https://www.tavinstitute.org/wp-content/uploads/2021/09/BELGIRATE-VII-BROCHURE_3-Sept.pdf

Belgirate VII Call for Papers. Available at https://akri.memberclicks.net/assets/Belgirate-Call-for-Papers.png

Berthoud, D.F., Kummel, P., Wagner, J., Erlich, S. & Marmorstein, J. (2023). Polyglossia or Babel? An exploration of authority, innovation, and identity in Group Relations Conferences. In C. Archer, R. Kelly, G. Strauss & J. Triest (Eds), *The Ecosystem of Group Relations: Culture, Gender and Identity in Groups and Organizations* (Chapter 9). Abingdon, UK: Routledge.

Gobry, P.-E. (2011, 4 May). 10 brilliant startups that failed because they were ahead of their time. *Business Insider.* Available at https://www.businessinsider.com/startup-failures-2011-5

Google Cloud. Language support. Available at https://cloud.google.com/translate/docs/languages

Green, Z.G. & Molenkamp, R.J. (2005). The BART system of group and organizational analysis. Available at https://www.akriceinstitute.org/assets/docs/free-papers/green%20and%20molenkamp%20-%202005%20-%20the%20bart%20system%20of%20group%20and%20organizational%20analys.pdf

Harkins, S., Bartlett, N., Hsu, Y.-K.K., Hsu, M.-H.D., Lu, X., Roth, J.D. & Wang, X. (2021). Group Relations in China: Portraits (Selfies) of Cross-cultural Study of Organizational Development 2014–2021. Belgirate VII.

Hayden, C. & Molenkamp, R.J. (2002). Tavistock Primer II. In S. Cytrynbaum & D. Noumair (Eds.). *Group Dynamics, Organizational Irrationality, and Social Complexity: Group Relations Reader 3.* A. K. Rice Institute.

Heffernan, V. (2010, 18 April). PharmVille. *New York Times Sunday Magazine.* Available at https://www.nytimes.com/2010/04/18/magazine/18fob-Medium-t.html

Heifetz, R. (1994). *Leadership Without Easy Answers.* Cambridge, MA: Belknap Press.

Hsiung, R.C. (2000). The best of both worlds: An online self-help group hosted by a mental health professional. *Cyberpsychology & Behavior*, *3*(6), 935–950.
Hsiung, R.C. (Ed.). (2002). *E-Therapy: Case Studies, Guiding Principles, and the Clinical Potential of the Internet.* W. W. Norton.
Kohn, N.V. & Roth, J.D. (2012). The blank screen of cyberspace. *Psychoanalytic Inquiry*, *32*(5), 426–437. DOI: 10.1080/07351690.2012.703565
Lipgar, R.M. (2007). Experiences in the first on-line Group Relations Conference: Lessons learned. ISPSO Annual Meeting. Available at https://ispso.org/Member-Resources-Post/experiences-in-the-first-on-line-group-relations-conference-lessons-learned
Manchin, A. (2010, 12 October). Entrepreneur mindset more common in U.S. than in EU, China. Gallup. Available at https://news.gallup.com/poll/143573/entrepreneur-mindset-common-china.aspx
Na, P, Jeste, D. & Pietrzak, R. (2022). Social disconnection as a global behavioral epidemic—A call to action about a major health risk factor. *Journal of the American Medical Association Psychiatry*. DOI: 10.1001/jamapsychiatry.2022.4162
Rogers, E.M. (1962). *Diffusion of Innovations*. New York: Free Press of Glencoe.
Roth, J.D. (2007). Director's report: On line Group Relations Conference. Unpublished.
Roth, J.D. (2008). Group Relations in Cyberspace. Kav Ofek. Available at http://ofek-groups.org/en/index.php?option=com_content&task=view&id=37&Itemid=59
Roth, J.D. & Tan, E.M. (2007). Analysis of an online Al-Anon meeting. *Journal of Groups in Addiction and Recovery*, *2*(1): 5–39.
Roth, J.D. & Tan, E.M. (2008). Spirituality and recovery from familial aspects of alcohol and other drug problems: Analysis of an online Al-Anon meeting. *Alcoholism Treatment Quarterly*, *26*(4): 399–426.
Storck, L.E. (2007, June). Continuous Online Group at the AGPA Annual Conference. *Contexts*, *36*: 38. Available at https://www.groupanalyticsociety.co.uk/CONTEXTS36.pdf
Venditto, V. (2020 Mar 25). It comes from China (video). Available at https://www.youtube.com/watch?v=KnX_iWAG6W4
Wikipedia (n.d.) Remain in Mexico. Available at https://en.wikipedia.org/wiki/Remain_in_Mexico
Wikipedia (n.d.). Web 2.0/ Available at https://en.wikipedia.org/wiki/Web_2.0
Wise, J. (2023). Members journey. Tavistock Community. Available at https://3.basecamp.com/3950600/buckets/12199430/messages/5730584284

10

Spotlighting corruption through the Group Relations lens

A selfie

Shmuel Erlich, Yael Shenhav Sharoni, Mira Erlich-Ginor, and Joseph (Yossi) Triest

Prologue and update

The event described in the present chapter took place in June 2018 and its write-up was completed in January 2023. In the course of this time, as the text was reaching its final version, a sociopolitical upheaval has taken place in Israel, aiming to revamp its established democratic system of government. In the wake of the last election, a prime minister on trial under criminal indictment, but nonetheless elected by a majority vote, appointed a team of senior ministers to his government, including, among others, one designated to be Finance Minister who had been convicted of bribery and repeated tax evasion, another, in charge of the police, who had been convicted of aiding and abetting Jewish terrorists, and yet another, effectively in charge of the occupied territories of Judea and Samaria, whose racist declarations and annexational designs were among the main reasons for his election by his supporters. In a manner difficult to digest, the first and central action of the new government, headed by one indicted and currently on trial, was directed at undermining the Supreme Court and passing a slate of laws intended to influence and subvert the judges and outcome of his trials, retroactively legitimising offences of which other leaders of the present regime had been convicted. If passed, it would confirm the right of criminally convicted persons to be elected to any and all government posts, and even to retroactively erase the court's ruling in their cases. Although the writing was on the wall when we held the event, it was difficult to believe at the time that what could be foreseen and predicted would actually take place. The great mystery which the event described below revolves around was and remains: how is it possible to understand the support and acceptance by a multitude – a majority, even if a narrow one, of Israeli public – of governmental corruption. We decided to bring what had transpired as it happened at the time of the event, and to let the reader draw the lines from it to what at the time was merely "the future".

Introduction

A "selfie" is a currently widespread mode of taking a picture of oneself, sometimes with a special background, at other times with special others. As in any

DOI: 10.4324/9781003502050-16

photographic activity, the most pertinent factors determining the picture's quality are focus and exposure time. This chapter takes *corruption* as its focus and tries not to lose it. Our exposure time is defined by the time boundaries of an experiential event conducted by OFEK with the aim of exploring the phenomenon of corruption through the combined lens of the psychoanalytic-systemic approach (an approach that combines psychoanalytic concepts and insights with group dynamics and open systems theory[1]) and Group Relations methodology.[2] You, our readers, are the viewers of this snapshot, with whom we share it in order to convey a multi-layered event and the story that emerged in it.

Background

Though corruption is never fully absent from any social scene, the last several years in Israel were heavily impacted by its shadow. The State's President, a prime minister, and the Chief Rabbi, as well as a couple of ministers, all ended in prison. The most recent item in this saga is the indictment of a long-reigning and well-known active prime minister on several counts of corruption, and his subsequent, still ongoing, trial. The public debate over his accountability and guilt nearly split Israeli society in two warring, bitterly opposed camps. The controversy played out against the additional backdrop of the COVID-19 pandemic and resulted in a political deadlock and four stalled elections in the space of two years.

The question that posed itself was therefore not *if* there is corruption but rather *how* it can be understood and explored, and *what* it represents for our society. These questions naturally affected us as citizens, but in OFEK (the Israel Association for the Study of Group and Organizational Processes) it stirred up the further question: can we utilise our GR methodology and tools to gain a better understanding of corruption? What can be learned from our experience that may be relevant and instructive for others?

With these questions in mind, the leadership of OFEK designed an event on the theme of corruption that would combine intellectual stimulation with experiential participation and group dynamics.

The design

The title given to the event was: "Corruption as a Social Symptom: Academia Meets Social Entrepreneurship". The primary task was defined as "Creating a learning space to understand corruption as a social phenomenon, using the tools of a psychoanalytic-systemic approach". The time frame was three and a half hours (including a break) from 18.00 to 21.30. The venue was a College of Management Academic Studies.

The design consisted of three parts: first, three presentations, representing three different areas of discourse; then an experiential event; and, finally, gathering what has emerged in the experiential event and the entire evening. Two OFEK members facilitated and managed the entire event.

Part 1. Presentations by representatives of three relevant disciplines

A psychoanalyst and founding member of OFEK focused on corruption as the social equivalent of individual paranoid breakdown (Erlich, 2013). Corruption is a symptom of group and social regression. Paranoid regression is characterised by a misinterpretation of perceived cues, leading to a breakdown of adequate, realistic judgement. The severance of reliable connections between perceived cues and their adequate interpretation leads to severe anxiety and regression, which culminates in a biased interpretation of reality, overwhelmed by projected fears, needs and wishes, which may give rise to violence and destruction. In parallel to such individual regression, at the social level this takes place when the links and connections between social values and social norms are undermined and destroyed. In such a context, corruption surfaces and is amplified, representing both the failure of normative behaviour and the undermining of the values which give rise to it, creating and fostering the fears and anxieties that ensue. Furthermore, individual, group, familial, and institutional paranoid regression are expressions of how power and authority are experienced and handled. Corruption is therefore a symptom of the social malaise that stems from the breakdown of the connection between values and norms.

A financial journalist, who is engaged in investigating corruption and heads the college's Social and Business track, presented several case illustrations of the way corruption has risen and spread in the current business world. Typically, it has to do with growing centralisation and control by a handful of people who are linked by family ties, friendship or reputation. The accumulation of power leads to ever larger ventures that require more capital than what is available, leading to borrowing and manipulating the banks on false premises, until eventually the flimsy structure collapses. Although much of this is well known and should have served as a deterrent, it is often disregarded due to personal greed and the feeling that one is immune because of one's special standing and power. Furthermore, this problematic chain of events is enabled by the tolerance that decent citizens display towards corruption at the highest echelons of business and government. The tendency is to minimise and dismiss it as insignificant when compared to actual performance, effectively resulting in tacit acceptance of greed and corruption. Ordinary citizens seem to be permissive about the unlawful behaviour of those in power, perhaps out of envy and identification. Finally, another factor promoting corruption is also the lack of sufficient deterrence by the courts to curb such greediness.

This last point leads directly to the third presentation by a professor of constitutional law. In her talk, she underscored the difference between what is legally clearly defined, representing the lowest minimal standard, below which it is considered legally forbidden and a *criminal* offence, as compared to *ethical* norms of behaviour, which represent values and aspirations, and occupy higher points on the scale. The problem is that such ethical norms are not clearly defined, and adherence to them rests on social acceptance, since they are not legally enforced or binding.

Between these two more or less clearly defined poles – the legally prohibited and the ethically aspired – stretches the grey expanse in which decent people conduct themselves more or less successfully, supported by varying degrees of social agreement. It is further obscured by the fact that different countries and societies deploy their ethical scales differently, leaving great gaps of unclarity as to what is permissible, appropriate or desirable behaviour. Public servants are particularly prone to usurp their power and need to be severely scrutinised and judged. All too often they tend to be preoccupied with personal gain and greed rather than with their service obligations. The courts are especially important and influential in this regard because they are able to uphold ethical standards. Yet they tend to be too lenient with public servants who are found guilty, employing legal rather than ethical standards, and commuting sentences rather than treating them severely as representing and shaping public normative behaviour, as some justices demand.

After a brief questions and answers period with the three presenters, the event moved to the second part, which was an experiential event.

Part 2. An experiential event: The World Café method

The World Café methodology is a simple, effective, and flexible format for hosting large group dialogue. It draws on seven integrated design principles, each of which has a specific purpose. It can be modified to meet a wide variety of needs. Specifics of context, numbers, purpose, location and other circumstances are factored into each event's unique invitation, design and question choice.[3]

The World Café method was chosen because it allows participants to express themselves briefly and openly while moving around fairly quickly, being exposed to some stimulating slogans, and mixing with others. It is a way to foster a lowering of guards and maximum dynamic involvement within a relatively short time span.

Nine round tables were set up, covered with red tablecloths and a flowerpot, creating a café ambiance. There was a host at each table who had received a set of instructions and remained at the table throughout this phase, while participants moved among the tables. Each table was equipped with a large sheet for drawing and writing and a stimulus slogan. The three slogans used were suggested by the three speakers. They represented frequently used phrases in contemporary discourse: *"Even if it happened, so what happened?" "Shame has died: Who or what killed it?"* and *"Why don't I intend to do anything about it?"* There were three 15-minutes rounds of shifting among the tables.

Part 3. The gathering stage

This phase consisted of collecting the themes that emerged at the different tables during the shifts, and a plenary discussion that included all participants, the three speakers and the two facilitators.

Emergent themes

The movement of people among the tables produced an atmosphere of lively participation and active involvement. While participants moved around, the three speakers remained on stage engaged in their own exchange, which enabled them to join the discussion from their vantage points and experience. The themes that emerged at the tables were recorded by the "anchors", i.e., the people who remained at the same table throughout, while the others moved and mixed. These emergent themes were subsequently introduced into the discussion and served to stimulate and elaborate associations and responses.

The general discussion gathered all the themes and provided a phase of continued lively exchange. Several themes emerged in the final discussion, which was lively and involved all participants. The thoughts, feelings and fantasies that emerged are presented here as the group's associations to the topic and to the stimulus questions and should be related to as such.

We summarise and outline below some of the major emergent themes, which fall into several intersecting categories.

Shame and the perception of the other

This theme emerged most powerfully and in direct response to the stimulating slogan: *"Shame has died, who killed it?"* It has been noted that the presence and impact of shame has not received sufficient attention in Group Relations conferences and literature (Short & Wagner, 2023). Shame can be a catalyst as well as an impediment to learning (Walker, 2017) and plays a significant role in any learning process (Brown, 2013).

In the present context, we could think of the impact of shame in terms of the metaphor of the selfie. As with a selfie, the perspective of the individual is quite circumscribed. It is limited to "from the individual" and "to the individual". Thus individualised self-centered perception is all important. In this self-centred state, who is the other? The other who is separate from me, who is looking at me critically, judgementally, and evaluatively has no place here, and does not exist *even as an imaginary other*. It is all about "me". The Self occupies the entire frame, leaving no space for the perception of the other and their vantage point. Shame, however, stems from perceiving oneself as viewed through the eyes and gaze of the other. Once the other is obliterated, the experience of shame is undermined and eradicated. And when shame is absent, there can be no inhibition, making it all right to take, to grab, even to steal.

In our present societal conditions, what happens in relation to the other has increasingly come under attack, simplification and erosion. The effect of the spread of virtual and remote discourse has been to erase the actual others that one relates to, to render them substance-less and dehumanised, with the direct consequence of not having to face and confront them physically. As one comment put it, "from Facebook to faceless". This virtuality of the other makes it possible to treat him/her as an effigy. In addition, it is frequently suffused with cynicism, contempt and hatred that are left hanging and unanswered. Everything happens in a virtual, detached, and unreal universe, where there is no responsibility or accountability. When the other remains faceless, usurping and taking what one desires is effectively unhindered. Thus, technological advances make for interpersonal cultural regression. It would be important to pursue this theme further, given the currently increasing resorting to remote meeting and interacting under the impact of the COVID-19 epidemic.

It is remarkable that one of the main slogans in the anti-government mass demonstrations in Israel is the crowd chanting in unison: "Shame!" It seems to be an attempt to restore the shame that has disappeared at the social level, whose deletion signifies the threat of disintegration.

Who is the victim?

Continuing the photographic metaphor, the *victim* of corruption is not "in the frame" and tends to be ignored as not sufficiently real or someone to be identified with. This theme seems to have been evoked by the stimulus question: "*Even if it happened, so what happened?*" Corruption often does not immediately and directly affect us as individuals. From the perspective of the group and social network, it tends to appear far removed and perhaps somewhat elusive. It is difficult to spot, identify and define, since it may not directly affect and concern us, and *there is no immediate victim we can identify with*. This absence of a victim one may identify with is a major difference between the *#MeToo* movement and corruption. In turn, this stance fosters distantiation and indifference. In addition, the issues surrounding corruption may appear abstruse and not available to internal evaluation by our symbolic thinking.

Individual vs. society

The individual's social presumption comes across as "everyone cheats, steals, and profits". Once this is the perceived norm, the individual feels it would be stupid for him not to behave in this way. If this is the norm, and everyone profits from it, why should I not profit as well? Furthermore, if I do not fall in line and I strike out against it, chances are that I may not survive. In this sense, the individual perspective of the social norm dictates doing what everyone else does, as in "when in Rome". The individual perception of the social collective is made up of countless individuals, all of whom act in the same way, share the same norms and values, and the pressure is on him to conform, or risk his viable existence and even perish.

Jewish history and cultural stance

The uniqueness of Jewish existence in the diaspora has permeated Israeli culture, shaping social values and norms in its image. The historical Jewish attitude towards formal state authority tended to see it as alien and condescending, an authority that must be tolerated and survived, and, if need be, can and should be circumvented, hoodwinked and cheated. In some cases, it even became important to "screw the authority" since it is wont to take advantage, abuse and forcefully fulfil its wishes. This attitude, which is still prevalent in Israeli society, implies that authority is not internalised and identified with, and must be circumvented in the interest of survival. This deep-seated paranoia fuels the existence and prevalence of corruption. In this sense, history repeats itself.

Can it change?

The discussion came around to asking how and what can be done to change these prevalent attitudes towards corruption, probably in response to the stimulus question: "*Why don't I intend to do anything about it?*" One recommendation that emerged, possibly in response to the World Café method, centred on the importance and value of working in small immediate groups. The feeling was that corruption signifies a social illness, and the remedy must consist of introducing and promoting change at the social level, which may best happen through small, intimate groups. It is worth noting that no grandiose or utopian notions emerged in the discussion. It was, rather, felt that small-scale working within one's immediate environment may spark and develop into greater critical masses, which in turn may lead to change in the social awareness of corruption and attending to this social illness.

Discussion

By conducting and sharing this event with its focus on corruption, we aimed to learn more about these issues and phenomena. A central question we wished to explore was: what may be the contribution of the psychoanalytic-systemic and Group Relations approach that we have adapted to this phenomenon? Although the event was not structured in any way as a Group Relations conference, we felt strongly that these perspectives informed and permeated it. Is this perspective justified, and what can be said about it?

A significant characteristic of the Group Relations perspective (encompassing the psychoanalytic-systemic approach) is the emphasis on exploring unconscious processes. We saw this as reflected, among others, in adopting a "listening perspective" or stance. In this event, it was evident that our listening (and, to a large extent, that of the participants) proceeded from the assumption that *unconscious themes* may emerge from the way the event was structured, and this in fact did happen. Furthermore, the unfolding of the event was characterised by a self-reflective stance that implied readiness to see oneself through the eyes of the other and to identify aspects of that otherness as one's own. This stance seems to have been enabled by several factors. Many participants had had Group Relations experience which they could and did draw on. The rest of the group lent itself readily to this mode of listening, which is characterised by attending to the unseen and unheard that is nonetheless present. An example that illustrates the way this approach manifested itself is the following. It was noted that the peripheral tables were poorly or not at all attended. This observation was interpreted as the unconscious enactment of the enormous differences between the centres and the periphery in the country. Similarly, most of the interventions offered looked for hidden meanings. The emotional tone was excited, lively and engaged (in no small measure due to the World Café method) and allowed for and enabled creativity to emerge. One illustration of this is two poems that were spontaneously recited, one by the youngest and one by the oldest participants.

There were further underlying assumptions at work that reflect Group Relations methodology and the psychoanalytic-systemic perspective. Notably, participants in this event at no time perceived themselves either as the perpetrators or direct victims of corruption, perhaps defensively so. Nonetheless, they regarded themselves as representatives of Israeli society, or at least of a particular social substratum. In our understanding, we employed a fractal model of representation, which regards every bit of the structure as repeating and representing the entire pattern or mould. Interventions were not only thoughtful, but interpretative, in an attempt to make sense of what emerged. Taken together, these various aspects of both the immersion in the process and what it brought up, and the efforts to make sense and learn from it, are, in our view, what gives this event the imprimatur of an application of the Group Relations approach.

The inclusion in this design of the three brief lectures may seem unrelated to the Group Relations approach, but this is not the case. It actually calls to mind the early versions of Group Relations conferences, in which lectures were often included and played a role. In our event it was evident that the lectures provided a multiple focus that served to stimulate and be part of the discussion. In addition, the three speakers were present throughout as a subgroup within the event. During the World Café, they interacted among themselves and later brought this into the general discussion. It is our view that the lectures provided a significant input and impetus for the event and served as a kind of "academic" link with the college venue in which it took place. The gathering process involved the entire group, including the speakers, as in a plenary, and allowed the themes to be raised and explored further.

Summary and conclusions

Conducting and presenting this event is, in our view, important for a number of reasons. Corruption is a widely spread social phenomenon and a symptom of social malaise, whether it occurs on a small or a large scale, and whether it receives much or little public attention. At the same time, corruption has not received the attention and understanding it deserves by prominent social theories and approaches, including that of Group Relations and the psychoanalytic-systemic approach. By initiating, designing and conducting this event against the poignant backdrop of widely spread and growing corruption in Israeli society, we feel we have contributed, albeit in a small way, to framing it as a phenomenon that needs to be observed, analysed, and treated. The event as we designed and carried it out provides a worthwhile general model for working on conscious as well as unconscious aspects of social issues in general, and on corruption in particular. The design presented here consisted of pulling together and integrating several techniques, ranging from academic-type input to an experiential component and their integrated exploration. Perhaps this design is not sufficiently coherent. One critical insight we have is that while we worked with the group as-a-whole and its coherence, we did not sufficiently allow for otherness to emerge – including the"'other within ourselves" – namely, where and how do we unconsciously contribute to the flourishing of corruption "outside". Perhaps the exclusion of the "corrupt other" – which was probably one of the reasons that little controversy emerged – calls for attention. Surely there are more crucial issues to be flagged, and this is also our aim in describing this work, so that it may be taken up and explored by others.

Notes

1 For the psychoanalytic-systemic approach see, for example, Gould et al. (2001). Open systems theory is best represented by Bertalanffy (1950).
2 For the Group Relations approach and methodology see Bruner (2006).
3 For further information on the World Café method, see https://www.involve.org.uk/resources/methods/world-cafe, and/or https://theworldcafe.com/key-concepts-resources/world-cafe-method/#.

References

Bertalanffy, L. von (1950). An outline of general systems theory. *British Journal of Philosophy & Science, 1*, 134–165.

Brown, B. (2013). *Men, Women, & Worthiness. The Experience of Shame and the Power of Being Enough.* Audible Audiobook. Sounds True.

Bruner, D. L. (2006). *Group Relations Conferences. Reviewing and Exploring Theory, Design, Role-Taking and Applications*. London: Karnac.

Erlich, H. S. (2013). Paranoia and regression in groups and organizations. In H. S. Erlich (Ed.), *The Couch in the Marketplace: Psychoanalysis and Social Reality* (pp. 123–131). London: Karnac.

Gould, L. J., Stapley, L. F. & Stein, M. (2001). *The Systems Psychodynamics of Organizations. Integrating the Group Relations Approach, Psychoanalytic, and Open Systems Perspectives*. New York: Karnac.

Short, E. L. & Wagner, J. K. (2023). In the shadow of envy. Shame in Group Relations Conferences. In C. Archer, R. Kelly, G. Strauss & J. Triest (Eds), *The Ecosystem of Group Relations. Culture, Gender and Identity in Groups and Organizations* (pp. 99–112). London: Routledge.

Walker, J. (2017). Shame and transformation in theory and practice of adult learning and education. *Journal of Transformative Education, 15*(4), 357–374.

Index

For Product Safety Concerns and Information please contact our EU representative GPSR@taylorandfrancis.com
Taylor & Francis Verlag GmbH, Kaufingerstraße 24, 80331 München, Germany

www.ingramcontent.com/pod-product-compliance
Ingram Content Group UK Ltd.
Pitfield, Milton Keynes, MK11 3LW, UK
UKHW020000200926
475702UK00015B/2393
* 9 7 8 1 0 3 2 8 1 2 6 1 8 *